IMAGES OF WAR

THE KAISER'S PANZERS

RARE PHOTOGRAPHS FROM WARTIME ARCHIVES

David Mitchelhill-Green

Greenhill Books

First published in Great Britain in 2025 by

Greenhill Books

c/o Pen & Sword Books Ltd, 47 Church Street, Barnsley,
South Yorkshire, S70 2AS, England
For more information on our books, please visit
www.greenhillbooks.com, email contact@greenhillbooks.com
or write to us at the above address.

ISBN 978-1-80500-179-9

A CIP catalogue record for this book is available from the British Library.

Typeset in Gill Sans by Concept, Huddersfield, West Yorkshire, HD4 5JL
Printed and bound in England by CPI Group (UK) Ltd, Croydon, CR0 4YY

Contents

Acknowledgements

My sincere appreciation is extended to the following individuals who generously shared their knowledge and images to make this book possible: Bertram Nold, David Charles Barlow and Tracy Dennis (National WWI Museum and Memorial, Kansas City, Missouri, USA). Many thanks to Michael Leventhal, from Greenhill Books, for championing history, Gwyn Evans for reviewing my manuscript and Noel Sadler for bringing the project to life.

Abbreviations

AIF	Australian Imperial Force
AKP 2	*Armee-Kraftwagen-Park* 2 (Army Transportation Depot No. 2)
AP	Armour piercing
AWM	Australian War Memorial
BAKP 20	*Bayerische Armee-Kraftwagen-Park* 20 (Bavarian Army Motor Vehicle Park 20)
hp	horsepower
km/h	kilometres per hour
mph	miles per hour
NARA	US National Archives and Records Administration
NAM	National Army Museum
OHL	*Oberste Heeresleitung* (Supreme Army Command)
VPK	*Verkehrstechnische Prüfungskommission* (Motor Transport Inspection Service)

Das Deutsche Kampfwagen-Abzeichen.

The German *Kampfwagenabzeichen* (tank badge) was a Weimar Republic decoration instituted by Otto Gessler, Minister of Defence, on 13 July 1921. It featured a Sturmpanzerwagen A7V on a battlefield, shrapnel shells bursting overhead, and was available privately to former crewmen of either an A7V or Beutepanzer (captured tank) who had participated in three assaults or were wounded in action. This book is the story of the Kaiser's Panzers – Imperial Germany's development and use of armour during the First World War.

Chapter One

An Armoured Fighting Vehicle

The concept of attacking an enemy with mobility and protection dates to biblical times with Assyrian chariots in 3,500 BC, Chinese war carts in 1,200 BC and protective towers atop elephants in 300 BC. Centuries later, Guido da Vigevano envisaged an armoured chariot as did Leonardo da Vinci, who wrote of 'building secure and covered chariots which are invulnerable, and when they advance with their guns into the midst of the foe, even the largest enemy masses must retreat; and behind them the infantry can follow in safety and without opposition.'

Harnessing steam power, English inventor James Cowen patented an armoured vehicle in 1855 based on a steam tractor. The subsequent invention of the internal combustion engine in the early 20th century ushered in a host of innovative designs. French Captain Léon René Levavasseur's 1903 design mirrored the modern tank. Sketched-out in a 1905 letter to France's Army Minister, Levavasseur's contraption was described 'an automobile field piece capable of covering all terrain accessible to harnessed vehicles and which ensures complete protection for personnel and powerplant against artillery fire and infantry bullets.' With wheeled vehicles confined to roads and favourable ground, the ability to traverse uneven territory finally arrived with Benjamin L. Holt's tracked tractor (Richard Edgeworth had earlier envisaged a caterpillar track in 1770, later developed and patented by Hornsby and bought by Holt), his first vehicle crawling off a US assembly line in 1909. Two years later in October 1911, Gunther Burstyn, an Austrian inventor and officer in the *Kaiserliche und Königliche Armee* (Austria-Hungarian Imperial and Royal Army), filed a patent for a Motorgeschütz ('motor gun'), an all-terrain tracked vehicle equipped with a turret and rapid firing cannon. Rejected in December 1911, Burstyn filed a patent in Germany on 28 February 1912 for an 'armoured vehicle, suitable for moving with its own motor power not only on roads but also on impassable terrain, characterized by sprung caterpillar tracks for locomotion, by wheels that can be raised and lowered for driving on roads, and by booms that enable the car to also cover wide trenches exceed.' With neither Vienna nor Berlin adopting Burstyn's concept, it was championed at the time by the German military periodical *Kriegstechnische Zeitschrift*. Discouraged, Burstyn lost interest in his project while the prospect of war in Europe edged closer.

Oberleutnant Gunther Burstyn, circa 1906. Born on 6 July 1879 in Bad Aussee, Austria, Burstyn retired from active military service in 1934 due to increasingly bad eyesight. Turning to anti-tank measures, he developed and patented a 'trap for combat vehicles' and later received a letter of recognition from General Heinz Guderian in 1940 plus the War Merit Cross with Swords 1st and 2nd Class, and 'honorary pay' for life. Through the intervention of his brother Walther, Burstyn personally presented his idea for a tank ferry to Adolf Hitler. He was later awarded an honorary doctorate from the Vienna University of Technology in 1944. On April 15, 1945, Burstyn committed suicide in Korneuburg, a few kilometres north of Vienna, which had just fallen to the Red Army.

A 1930s model of Burstyn's Motorgeschütz. According to his German patent, a three-man crew would comprise a commander and loader (front right), gunner (front left) and, curiously, a driver sitting with his back to the direction of travel. Specifications: length 3.5m (minus boom); width 1.9m; height 1.9m; combat weight approximately 7 tons, powerplant: 45hp petrol engine; projected spend: road 28.8km/h, cross country 8km/h; armour: front 8mm, rear and side armour 4mm; armament 3.7cm rapid-fire cannon and two machine guns.

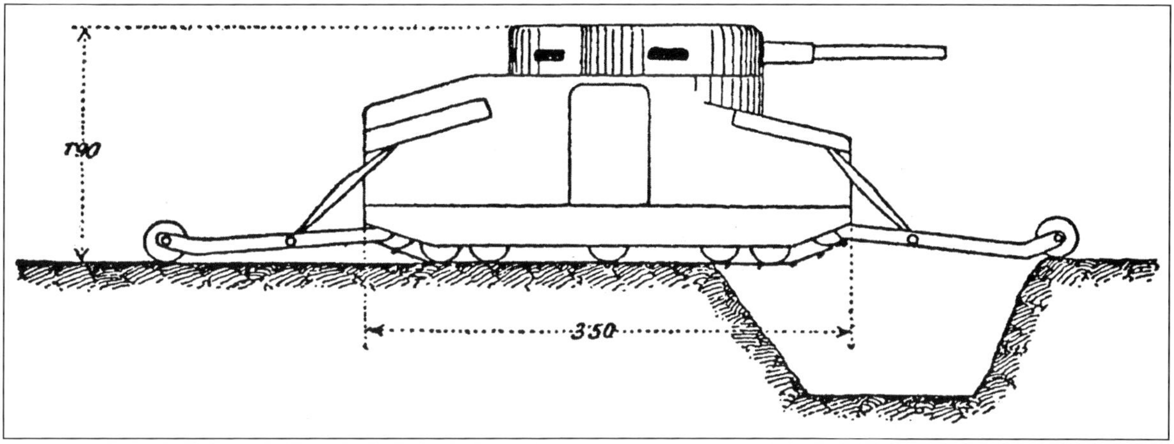

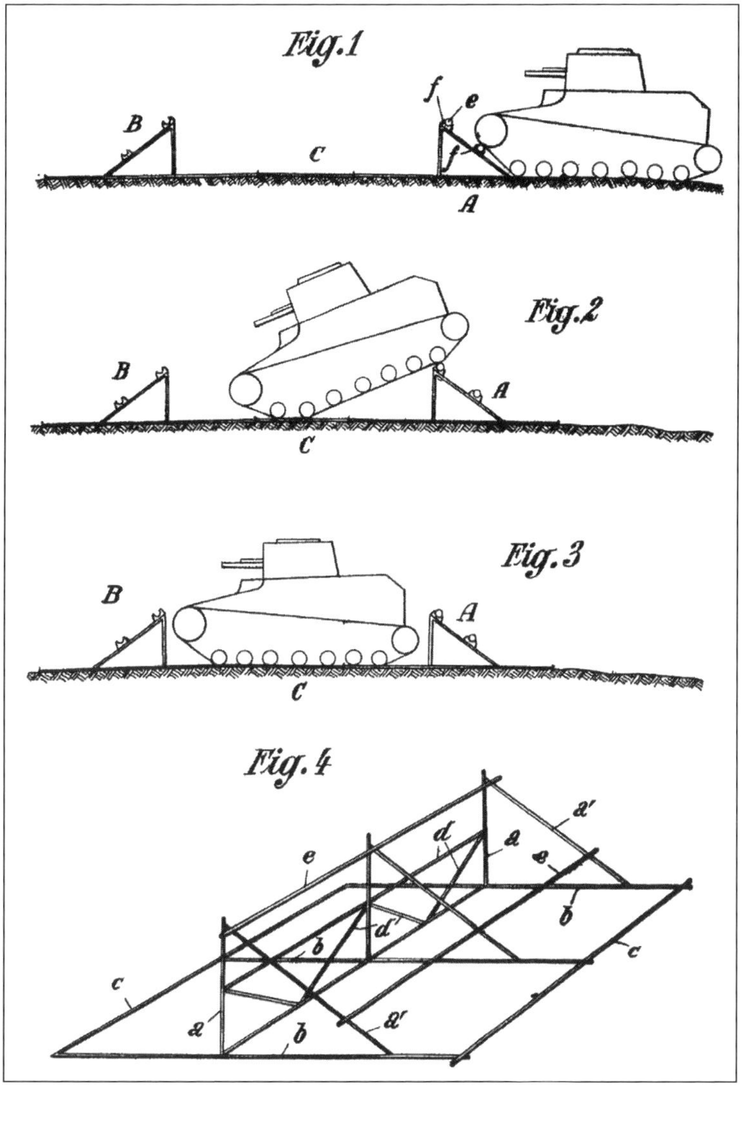

Retractable booms, what Burstyn called 'arms', with wheels would assist the Motorgeschütz cross trenches and ditches. In 1924 Burstyn refuted the 'claim that the Kampfwagen is an English invention' writing, 'the term "tank" should be avoided, being a foreign word and technically incorrect', though appearing in various newspapers and journals. 'This claim is completely wrong', he refuted. 'This judgment [for his invention] was made by the authority in this area, the Patent Office, when I, in 1911, applied for a patent for the Kampfwagen. Back then I called it Motorgeschütz.'

Turning his hand to anti-tank obstacles, Burstyn patented a tank trap in Germany in 1935.

Burstyn was not alone, as a later German report noted, for 'there was no lack of various kinds of suggestions, as our industry was flourishing and there were not only inventors but also financiers.' Heinrich Ehrhardt's Ballonabwehr-fahrzeug (Balloon defense vehicle) featured a 5cm L/30 anti-balloon gun on a partially armoured 1906 Opel truck.

Mirroring Burstyn's experience, Australian engineer Lancelot de Mole's advanced concept of a 'caterpillar fort' was rejected by the British War Office in 1912. Although friends suggested that he approach the German consul in Western Australia, de Mole steadfastly refused on the grounds that Germany might one day be an enemy: 'If my own country doesn't want my brains, I'm not going to sell them to a beastly foreigner.' Plagued by poor health, de Mole was accepted into the Australian Army in 1917. Together with Lieutenant Harold Boyce (later to become Sir Harold Boyce and Lord Mayor of London), who financed the manufacture of a 1/8th scale model, the two men sailed for London on a troopship, their vehicle mock-up under constant guard. Arriving in Plymouth in January 1918, de Mole obtained duty leave and presented his design to Britain's Munitions Inventions Office. Ill health again intervened and

Also spurned by Germany and Austria, Daimler engineers, led by Robert Wolf, received permission to sell their four-wheel drive Panzerautomobile to France. Despite a reasonable off-road capability and the ability to climb a 60-degree incline, the vehicle was ultimately eschewed by the *Commission d'Étude des Armes Portatives et de Petit Calibre* in a 1909 report that criticised armoured cars for poor off-road performance and high production costs. Interestingly, among those who inspected the Daimler vehicle was Archduke Franz Ferdinand of Austria.

de Mole was unable to demonstrate his model to a second committee. His model was now languishing in a government basement and his correspondence pigeon-holed. With the launch of the German Spring offensive in 1918, de Mole was called back to active service where he fought at Meteren, Merris, and Villers-Bretonneux.

Lancelot de Mole's idea was inspired by the uncomfortable experience of travelling of over rough country terrain in Western Australia. As he explained, the proposed vehicle 'can be steered to the right or left, when proceeding forwards, by altering the direction that the chain-rail is laid in by screwing the front portions to one side or the other … or steered, when proceeding backwards, by pressing the bogie nearest the rear end of the tank to one side by means of the screw gear … or a hydraulic ram controlled by the steersman, thereby causing the body of the vehicle to be thrown to the right or left as required so that, as the vehicle proceeds, the links of the chain will be laid to the right or left of the line that the vehicle has been proceeding on and so form a curve, which as the vehicle proceeds will alter the direction of travel.' (AWM J00300)

Unsuccessful in lodging a claim with a British royal commission rewarding inventors for their contribution to the war effort, Britain's postwar Tank Commission was more receptive, acknowledging: 'We consider that he is entitled to the greatest credit for having made and reduced to practical shape as, far back as the year 1912 a very brilliant invention which anticipated and, in some respects, surpassed that actually put into use in the year 1916. It was this claimant's misfortune, and not his fault, that his invention was in advance of his time and failed to be appreciated and was put aside because the occasion for its use had not then arisen.'

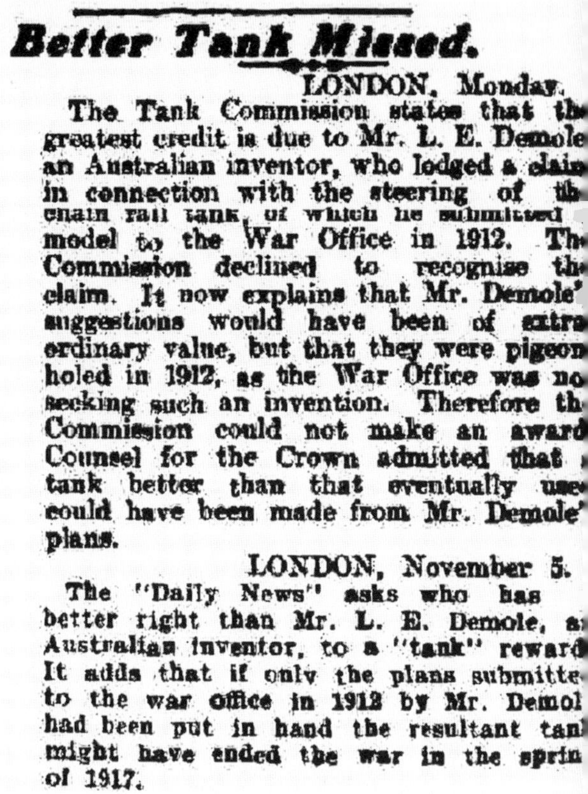

Better Tank Missed.

LONDON, Monday.

The Tank Commission states that th greatest credit is due to Mr. L. E. Demole an Australian inventor, who lodged a clai in connection with the steering of th chain rail tank, of which he submitted model to the War Office in 1912. The Commission declined to recognise th claim. It now explains that Mr. Demole' suggestions would have been of extra ordinary value, but that they were pigeon holed in 1912, as the War Office was no seeking such an invention. Therefore th Commission could not make an award Counsel for the Crown admitted that tank better than that eventually use could have been made from Mr. Demole' plans.

LONDON, November 5.

The "Daily News" asks who has better right than Mr. L. E. Demole, a Australian inventor, to a "tank" reward It adds that if only the plans submitte to the war office in 1912 by Mr. Demol had been put in hand the resultant tan might have ended the war in the sprin of 1917.

Another failed pre-war design. Like Germany, Britain had failed to initiate a means of transporting artillery or supplies over rough terrain or stay abreast of developments in armoured motorised firepower. Richard Simms' 'War-Car', seen here at London's Crystal Palace in 1902, failed to arouse interest in Britain's War Office. A second pre-war British armoured car, designed by Walter Wilson, likewise failed to garner interest. Wilson would later play a major role in the development of Britain's first tank.

Chapter Two

'This strange creature, with its steel hide impenetrable to bullets'

During the first days of August 1914, it 'rained ultimatums and declarations of war', British Lieutenant Colonel Charles à Court Repington, an influential war correspondent, declared in his memoirs:

> ... very soon all the great Powers of Europe, except Italy, were at war. Though war had often been expected, it had been expected for so long, and so many crises had been successfully overcome by diplomacy, that in the end it came like a thief in the night.'

Few had foreseen the 'possibility of the static warfare which lasted on the Western Front for nearly four years', recalled Major General Ernest Swinton, who played a seminal part in Britain's development and adoption of the tank. 'We now know that the Germans had no more expected protracted trench warfare than had the French or we ourselves.' Solutions were sought to overcome enemy troops manning miles of trenches behind barbed wire entanglements with zones of advance swept by rifle and machine gun fire. One solution was massed artillery bombardments, which quickly churned the landscape into a heavy contested quagmire impassable to wheeled vehicles. While Germany introduced chemical warfare – poison gas and the flame thrower – Entente Powers turned to developing an armoured tracked armoured vehicles to break the bloody deadlock of trench warfare.

Having witnessed the carnage on the Western Front as a war correspondent, Swinton was determined to seek a solution to the stalemate on the Western Front. He recorded that 'our efforts to advance ... in most cases [were] frustrated by machine guns, frequently in combination with an obstacle hastily made from rabbit wire or fencing'. To circumvent the problem, he pictured a mechanical solution – an 'armoured vehicle immune against bullets, which should be capable of destroying machine guns and of ploughing a way through the wire'. Swinton's 1915 proposal by

German solders train with a flame-thrower. This weapon was first used against French troops outside Verdun on 26 February 1915.

Exploiting a loophole in international law proscribing the use of asphyxiating gas, Germany first used projectors to release chlorine gas from cylinders at the northern end of the Ypres salient on 22 April 1915.

Britain's prototype tank, officially known as His Majesty's Land Ship (HMLS) *Centipede* and christened 'Mother', during trials at Lincoln. It was subsequently demonstrated before Lord Kitchener, Secretary of State of War, David Lloyd George, Minister of Munitions (and future prime minister), and Reginald McKenna, the Chancellor of the Exchequer, at Hatfield Park on 2 February 1916. A separate demonstration for King George V six days later prompted Tennyson d'Eyncourt afterwards to pen an enthusiastic report to Churchill. This resulted in an order for 100 'tanks'.

British for 'Armoured Machine Gun Destroyers to overcome the [Western Front] impasse', using an American-designed Holt tractor or similar caterpillar system, was encouraged by Winston Churchill, then First Lord of the Admiralty.

The Western Front was mired in blood. And controversy. Already between August 1914 and December 1915, the British Expeditionary Force had sustained some 375,000 battlefield casualties. General (later Field Marshal) Sir Douglas Haig, Commander-in-Chief of the British Expeditionary Force, launched his Somme offensive on 1 July 1916, hoping to pierce the German line. It proved disastrous. Casualties on the opening day were the greatest sustained by any army in a single day – 57,470, of whom 20,000 died. His armies, in time, would suffer more than 400,000 casualties for no significant gain. Officially trialled on 2 February 1916, the tank was an option

Haig seized upon to sustain his offensive. Counter to Swinton's requirements for successful deployment, insufficiently trained crews in forty-nine Mark I tanks were thrust into combat for the first time at the Battle of Flers-Courcelette (two villages in the German defensive line), on 15 September 1916 as part of the much larger Somme offensive.

The first tanks set off in the wake of an artillery barrage. Captain Harold Mortimore's Mark I, No. 765 (D Company), dubbed *Daredevil*, was the first tank to see action. 'I managed to get astride one of the German trenches in front of the wood and opened fire', he recalled. 'There were some Germans in the dugouts and I shall never forget the looks on their faces when they emerged and saw my tank'. Arnold Ridley (actor and playwright of *Dad's Army* fame) from the Somerset Light Infantry was among the accompanying infantry, later writing: We in the ranks had never heard of tanks. We were told that there was some sort of secret weapon and then we

Mark I male No. 741/ C15 in action on 15 September 1916.). Note the raised 'tail'. Weighing 28 tons, with a crew of eight, the vehicle could reach 3.7mph. Lacking a turret, the two 6-pounder guns were mounted in separate side sponsons. The long barrel, however, was easily clogged traversing steeply undulating ground or damaged should the machine strike trees or other obstacles. An Australian soldier serving in a tank later wrote of his experience in tank, 'a strange sensation, worse than being in a submarine. Suddenly a terrible lurch. We are astride an enemy trench. "Give them hell", was the order. Our guns raked the trenches right and left, and the Huns were shot down in branches like scared rabbits. The experience was not altogether pleasant. Tank sickness is as bad as sea sickness.'

British Mark 1 tank, D1 *Daredevil*, No.765, sits disabled on the battlefield. After a five-minute delay, the tank advanced on Delville Wood at 5.15am. After clearing several trenches, it was stopped after an enemy shell struck the left track. The rhomboid shape would remain the standard hull design of British tanks throughout the war. In the absence of a muffler, engine noise, even flames passed through open exhausts through the tank's roof. Observation from inside the tank was difficult, rendering and efficient fire control almost impossible. (AWM P00826.001)

saw this thing go up the right-hand corner of Delville Wood. I saw this strange and cumbersome machine emerge from the shattered shrubbery and proceed slowly down the slope towards Flers'. It would be as fearsome to the German soldier as Pyrrhus' 'secret weapon' – twenty war elephants on loan from Ptolemy II of Egypt – was to the ancient Romans.

Despite receiving rumours and intelligence reports of a new Allied weapon, Leutnant Otto Schulz, Westphalian infantry, was nevertheless shocked by the appearance of the first British tanks. 'When we saw the first real tank it was like nothing we had ever imagined', he exclaimed. Until now, the machine gun had reigned as the undisputed holder of no-mans land. But as Schulz's men discovered, 'we got nothing from the tanks but sparks.' Pushing through barbed wire barricades with apparent ease, and invincibility, a soldier shouted: 'the Devil is coming'. 'One stared as if one had lost the power of one's limbs', a German prisoner later attested after his first encounter with a tank, 'The big monsters approached us slowly, hobbling, rolling, rocking, but always advancing.' Retiring to new defensive lines, a new word emerged: *Tankschrecken* (tank horror).

The British Mark 1 male (No. 721) C5 *Crème de Menthe* was among the first tanks in combat. Note the terrain churned up from earlier barrages and the loss of one of its rudder-like steering wheels, a feature prone to failure and later deleted in November 1916. Naming convention for British tanks saw them classified as 'male' or 'female'. A shortage of the 'long' Hotchkiss 6-pounder guns, due to Royal Navy requirements, for 'male' vehicles led to the manufacture of the machine-gun-only 'female' tanks armed with four .303-inch Vickers machine guns in sponsons (fixed turrets on each side) and a single forward-facing, air cooled 303-inch Hotchkiss machine gun. It was also thought, in the absence of case shot ammunition, that the machine gun variants would help stop German infantry from storming the vehicles. 'This ingenious and mysterious wobbler', a private Aspland later explained to the *Sunday Times*, 'mystifying and horrifying Fritz, [it] has many names, the most popular being tank, caterpillar, juggernaut, and ichthyosaurus. The monster charged and "led" the men down High-street at Flers.'

Although still experimental and dogged by various challenges, the first tanks marked a breakthrough in military technology. Britain's press stirred public imagination, lauding the new weapon. Phillip Gibbs, one of five official war correspondents with the British Army, wrote of troops 'exalted and excited by the smell of victory'. Gibbs detailed the success of a leading tank, C5 *Crème de Menthe,* under the command of Arthur Inglis, Gloucestershire Regiment:

> They were enormously cheered and amused by the new weapon . . . The secret of these extraordinary, armoured motors has been jealously kept for months. All manner of marvellous powers are attributed to them. They are proof against bullets, bombs, and shell splinters, and take ditches like kangaroos. The actual sight of them was monstrously comical. They are like enormous toads, and the only effect on the inquisitive troops was shouts of laughter. But they did good work and scared the Germans dreadfully . . . The troops cheered and shouted encouragement, and even laughed, with blood-streaming faces. The creature named *Crème de Menthe* waddled forward over the old German trenches and went forward steadily toward the redoubt. The enemy was momentarily silent. Then spasms of machine-gun fire splashed at the *Crème de Menthe*'s sides but fell harmlessly. The *Crème de Menthe* advanced upon the broken wall and leaned against it. The bricks crashed down, and the motor walked into the heart of the factory ruins. The motor poured out a stream of bullets, trampled down machine-gun emplacements, crushed machine-guns, killed teams of infantry, and followed up and occupied the redoubt. Similar scenes took place at High Wood. Our men for a time were driven back. Then there was great joy at seeing several 'tanks' advancing through the wood, and on each side wounded soldiers relate extraordinary stories. They declare that the 'tanks' broke down trees, mounted barricades, and stamped out dug outs. The Boches, thoroughly scared, ran about shouting as if demented.

Rhetoric aside, it was an inauspicious debut for Britain's Mark I tank. Manufacturing delays were exacerbated by track failure, due to a 50-mile design life (already worn from training) and ill-prepared drivers. Of the forty-nine vehicles shipped to the Somme, seventeen succumbed to breakdowns or becoming ditched, leaving thirty-two machines spread across the starting line. Of this number, only nine managed to push ahead of the infantry, causing considerable German casualties. Another nine failed to keep up with the infantry, though succeeded in mopping up enemy positions. Of the remaining fourteen tanks, nine were beset with mechanical problems; five were ditched.

Failing to satisfy Churchill and Swinton's expectations with a decisive victory on a challenging battlefield, the Mark I tank had nevertheless showcased its potential for

(**Above**) Burnt out British Mark I male, C23 *Clan Ruthven*, abandoned near Picardy. A German army report from 20 October 1916 claimed three English tanks were destroyed by German artillery. Although these first vehicles failed to impress the officers of the Supreme Army Command, discussion nevertheless commenced at the end of the month regarding the potential usefulness of such a weapon.

(**Opposite**) The *New York Times* (7 January 1917) reported on an immobilised Mark I tank that was overrun after penetrating the German line. 'When the Germans found this strange creature, with its steel hide impenetrable to bullets, stalled, curiosity and a desire for revenge were a fillip to their courage. They went after it with the avidity of prehistoric man stalking a wounded mammoth whose bulk was fast in one of the alleys of the cave dwellers. No such game was ever seen on this western front, marked as it has been by all kinds of bizarre fighting. According to the accounts given by the British officers with veracious solemnity, while the tank's machine guns blazed right and left, some of the Germans managed to creep along the trenches under the forelegs and hindlegs of the crouching beast. Then they swarmed over it, looking for an opening through which to strike at its vitals. They fired their rifles into joints and bombed it all over, but to no more avail than burglars trying to reach the inside of a battleship with a jimmy. All the while the tank's machine guns kept busy at the human targets within reach, while its crew, chosen daredevils, concluded to stick until they starved, or the Germans found the proper can opener to get them out. Finally, the British infantry in the rear, seeing the tank in distress, refused to wait on any General's orders that they should remain at the objective which they had gained. They were out to save that impounded tank, and with a cheer they rushed the Germans and overwhelmed them. When the crew heard the laughing and shouting in English, they opened the door and called out: "We are all right if you will only get us one more juice, so that the old girl can have a guzzle of her proper drink, and we can take the road again." So the infantry formed a line in front of the tank, determined to defend her to the last man, while a runner was hurried back for a can of gasoline. The gasoline arrived safely, and the beast, having taken a swallow, ambled back into reserve amid wild cheering. It left behind 250 dead Germans, according to its commander.'

Another overwhelmed Mark I, No. 548, D13, *Delilah*. Britain's press was quick to denounce German accusations that the 'tank' breached international rules of warfare. (AWM H02113)

German drawing of a British tank after the first encounter. Vizefeldwebel Tauscher, 104th Infantry Regiment, reported on the novel weapon: 'It is very elongated, not tubby nor shaped like an egg. The bow projects noticeably ahead of the wheels. The side surfaces of the body are vertical and are not curved; the rear end is also flat and is closed by means of a door. One of the members of the crew left the vehicle, walked for a short time behind it and got back in. Below the body there are fixed sledge-runners which project on the right and left ahead of the wheels. The front wheels are between 1.50 and 1.70m high and are located in approximately the first third of the body. The rims are not flat but have projections on them so that from the side they look like cogwheels. If one wheel slips into a shell hole or if the vehicle drives over a trench (it easily crossed a very deep gap 1.50m wide) then the vehicle rests on the runners and the wheel or the rear- wheels push the body, resting as it is on the tracks, far enough forward for the driving wheels to be able to grip again.'

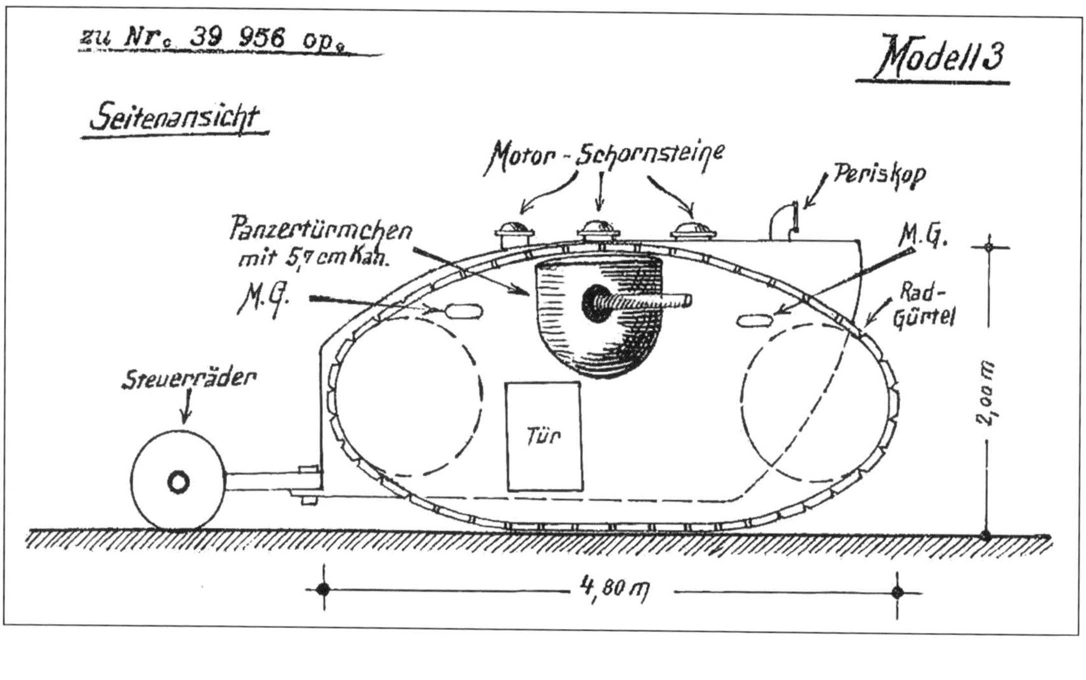

Mark I male, C 19, *Clan Leslie*. Buoyed by the weapon, an Australian Corporal penned a letter to his parents in October 1916, writing that 'since the introduction of tanks, land-dreadnoughts on caterpillars, Fritz has started to whine piteously, [claiming] that this new innovation is not warfare but downright butchery and murder. One [smiles] at his dilemma now "the tables have turned."' On the other side, a German newspaper correspondent reported: 'When the German outposts crept out of their dugouts in the mist of the morning and stretched their necks to look for the English, their blood was chilled in their veins. Mysterious monsters were crawling towards them over the craters. Stunned as if an earthquake had burst around them, they all rubbed their eyes, fascinated by the fabulous creatures.'

tactical support, drawing fire from the infantry, reducing the machine-gun's dominance, surmounting enemy strongpoints and demoralizing German infantry. A modicum of mobility returned to the battlefield with invaluable lessons learnt, including the need for careful planning and reconnaissance thorough training and adequate communication. Increased mechanical reliability, speed and thicker armour would be needed for future tanks to deliver a decisive result. Haig nevertheless expressed confidence in the machine, declaring: 'Wherever the tanks advanced, we took our objectives and where they did not advance, we failed to take our objectives. Go back and make as many more tanks as you can.' Back in Britain, not all senior officers were so convinced of the vehicle's future, which hung in the balance. Citing defects, an order for 1,000 placed by Haig's representative on 19 September 1916 was rescinded on 10 October. Doggedly determined, Major Albert Stern appealed to Lloyd George, then Minister of War, who promptly reinstated effectively what was an

The War Illustrated, 9th December, 1916. Page 396 Page 397 The War Illustrated, 9th December, 1916.

Mysterious Monsters on the Muddy Somme: Land-Cruisers Luffing into the Battle Line

Canadian War Records

Official Photographs

Crash against the enemy, the "tank" goes into action with something of the bravado of a medieval knight in armour. A monster of living steel, it churns its way over obstacles and into positions with a blind, implacable fury that recognises no obstacles.

A mail-coated leviathan spitting fire as it goes. A "tank" crawling over the desert of war steered by its invisible crew, whose bravery is akin to that of submarine men bringing their craft into position during a naval action.

While the "tanks" caused roars of laughter from Britons who witnessed the first move into action, the Germans suffered a painful surprise, and, in many cases utterly demoralised by the steely and apparently invulnerable novelty, surrendered en masse.

Craters and shell-holes to the landship are like so many waves to a powerful destroyer. The "tank" weathers them all with an imperturbability which is sometimes as comic to those behind it as it is tragic to those who have to face the onslaught.

War Illustrated announced the arrival of the 'tank', a 'mail-coated leviathan', possessing the 'bravado of a medieval knight in armour.'

open-ended order believed to have reached 405 male and 610 females, 205 tender or supply tanks, eleven experimentals and fifty-four surplus vehicles.

Rumours abounded about Germany's reaction. It was argued in a London masthead, with a sense of pride, that the enemy will undoubtedly 'devise even bigger monsters and achieve more horrific results. But they will not deprive us of the honour of being first in the field with these bullet-spitting creatures of steel.' British armoured warfare theorist, Brevet-Colonel John Frederick Charles Fuller (known by his initials J.F.C.), was likewise convinced that the Germany would introduce a heavy tank because of the situation on the Western Front and considering the 'characteristic of the German mind towards inventions'. Whereas the 'Germans are a thoughtful race', Fuller contended, 'they are not imaginative, consequently anything which strikes their imagination and awakes it fascinates them – colossal monuments, colossal airships anything which from the point of view of power will awaken the brute within them.' Reuters quoted a Cologne newspaper with news of a 'Land cruiser' superior to British 'tanks', which were deemed to be 'too slow, and not heavily enough armoured.'

As early as June 1915 British intelligence in France drafted a disquieting commentary (of questionable provenance) on a purported new German design:

> It has been reported that Krupp's are about to produce a large and powerful high-speed car capable of going at high speed over rough ground. It is described as dispersing over a zone of 100 metres some burning gas of such intensity that everything is destroyed within its radius. Experiments are said to have proved successful and a number of these cars are said to be turned out. The car is said to be heavily armoured so that only a heavy shell could damage it. Krupp's workmen are informed that it is to be used simply for burning the dead.

Still, this was possibly the first warning London received of enemy tank development. 'Neutral travellers', London's *Times* correspondent in Amsterdam later reported in January 1917, were adamant that Krupp was 'working day and night producing tanks and other novelties. They say that surprises may appear in the new offensive.' Writing in the *Sunday Pictorial* two months later, journalist James Douglas predicted how the 'battles of 1917 will be battles of tanks as well as battles of guns and aeroplanes':

> I picture thousands of tanks in action. The German tanks will make their debut, for the Germans are prompt copyists. I have no doubt that they will try to provide tank destroyers. But we have secured the advantage of the initiative. And the tank is the weapon of the attacker, rather than that of the defender. His function is to complete the havoc wrought by high explosives. A stationary tank is only an armoured house. Moreover, a tank on the defensive cannot quickly be transferred to another point. Tanks cannot be used like machine guns. The enemy cannot stud his whole front with tanks.

23rd December, 1916.

No. 123. Vol. 5.

THE WAR *Illustrated*

A PICTURE-RECORD *of Events by Land, Sea and Air.* *Edited by* J. A. HAMMERTON

TOASTING THE "TANK."—This machine is comparatively a new-comer into the arena of battle, but as the gladiator on his entrance into the Colosseum was toasted and cheered by his supporters, so this extraordinary symbol of modern mechanical power may appropriately be toasted by the heroes of the Somme whom it precedes "over the top," through shell-hole and barbed-wire, to victory.

December 1916 and a toast to the tank, a 'new-comer into the arena of battle'

German Armoured Cars

Germany had largely overlooked pre-war testing of armoured cars, dismissing their tactical value. Consequently, the Kaiser's army lacked armoured vehicles when it went to the war on 28 July 1914. This would be a short war, his generals felt, one that would be quickly won after a decisive thrust through France. The use of captured Belgian Minerva armoured cars just months into the conflict, however, may have persuaded *Oberste Heeresleitung* (Supreme Army Command, or OHL) to reconsider its position with a call for an armoured reconnaissance vehicle issued In October 1914. Prototypes were subsequently presented by Büssing, Daimler and Ehrhardt in Düsseldorf and Zella-Mehlis.

The Belgian Minerva armoured car. German forces captured four early 1914 model cars, which they employed during the invasion of Romania. At least one vehicle saw service in Berlin after the war during the 1919 uprising.

The Büssing AG A5P was a large four-wheel drive vehicle powered by a 90hp engine and bristling with machine gun ports. With a crew of ten, six men operated the three machine guns through ten available hatches. Judged inferior to the Ehrhardt design, production ceased after the third vehicle was completed.

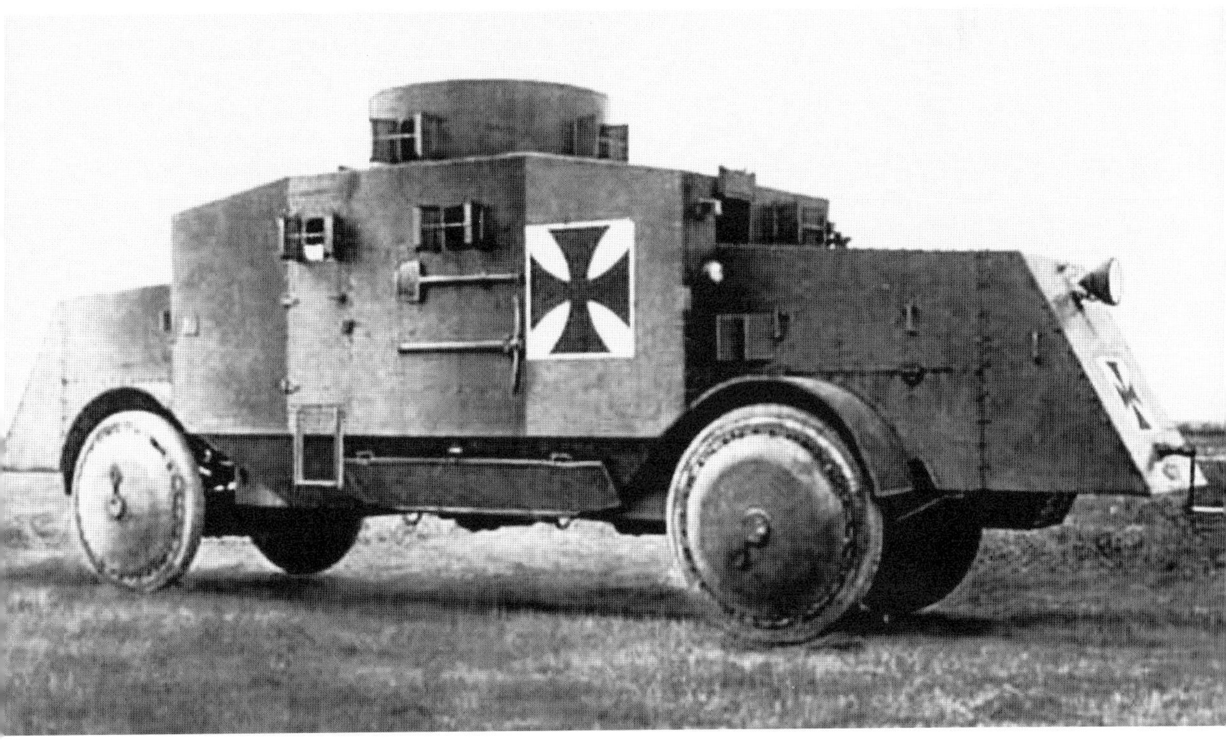

(**Above**) Daimler's Model 1915 also fulfilled the all-wheel drive requirement. It was basically a Daimler truck protected by a slab-sided armoured superstructure, armed with three Maschinengewehr 08 (MG 08) machine guns.

(**Below**) The German MG 08, a water cooled, fully automatic weapon, was capable of firing up to 500 rounds per minute of 7.92mm belt-fed ammunition. (AWM RELAWM29353.001)

(**Opposite, above**) Ehrhardt's E-V/4 Straßenpanzerwagen, seen here in Russia, incorporated lessons learned from all earlier prototype vehicles, chiefly the need to reduce weight, provide a turret capable of rotating, armoured vision ports, headlamp protection and enclosed rear wheels. Although a large vehicle, the interior became cramped when carrying a normal crew of eight or nine men. Unable to traverse the muddy terrain of the Western Front, it was decided in 1916 to combine all available armoured cars into the 1st Panzerkraftwagen MG Platoon and transfer them to the Romanian front with the Schmettow Cavalry Corps where mobile warfare on paved and unpaved roads was still possible. Their success convinced OHL to order further vehicles, though with Büssing and Daimler already engaged in war-related projects the contract was awarded solely to Ehrhardt, who produced thirty-three examples.

(**Opposite, below**) Although intended for use on roads, the Ehrhardt E-V/4 featured four-wheel drive and a six-speed gearbox (six forward and reverse gears). A radio with a tall, extendable aerial proved unpopular and was removed.

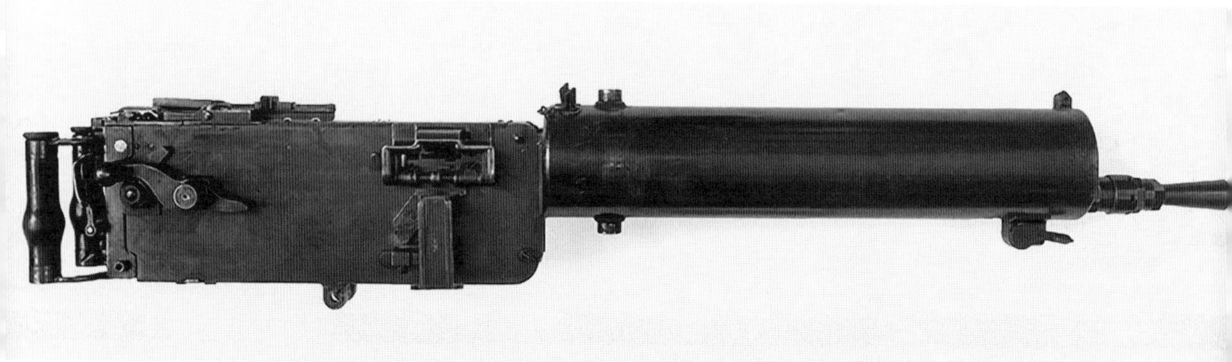

ИЧА СЕВР

Ehrhardt E-V/4s equipped the 2nd, 3rd, 4th, 5th and 6th Panzerkraftwagen-MG platoons. These newly formed units were successfully used on the Romanian and Ukrainian fronts, and later in Alsace and on the Italian front. Some units also supported the German spring offensive of 1918 on the Western Front, though with significantly higher losses. Towards the end of 1917, another twenty examples were ordered, some of which served in Freikorps units after the 1918 Armistice.

Chapter Three

'The enemy succeeded in achieving a surprise attack'

Britain's next major use of armour, though not on the scale predicted by Douglas Haig, began on Easter Monday, 9 April 1917. Planning called for tanks to assist infantry in breaking through the Hindenburg Line outside Arras. In the absence of the newer Mark IV tanks, which had failed to arrive in time, the sixty machines allocated to the offensive comprised forty-five Mark II training tanks and fifteen surviving Mark I machines. Challenged by appalling weather and a veritable sea of mud, 'nobody was pleased to hear the heavy rain that fell', a British tanker later wrote, 'as we knew the ground was bad enough without that to make it worse.' The use tanks of this occasion impressed neither the accompanying Australian infantry nor the German defenders. With overnight snow concealing white guide tapes, tanks became lost and arrived late. An Australian report 'on co-operation of "tanks" – night of 10/11 April 2017' was especially critical.

> The tank co-operation in the attack made on the Hindenburg Line on the night of 10/11 April 1917 was useless or worse than useless ... Tanks were late in arriving at rendezvous, which means that they were late in getting to the jumping off place. In fact, only three got to the latter place at all. Of the six tanks allotted to the Brigade, five reached rendezvous; one being out of action before that place was reached ... The tanks crews seemed to know little or nothing of an attack by infantry or nothing whatsoever about the particular operation they were to participate in. For instance, in the case of No. 2 tank, the tank commander had not even synchronised his watch; his time being five minutes behind true time as given to the infantry. Further, tank crew did not even know the direction of enemy up to their objectives ... they opened fire on our own troops thereby causing many casualties. One tank in particular opened on our men in the jumping off place, killing four, and wounding others...In my opinion, tanks manned by the bravest of crews and placed directly under the Infantry Officers concerned in operations would be of great help but they should never be relied upon as the sole arm of support in an attack by infantry. In our case,

> not a shot was fired when tanks were taking up their positions so the whole operation was given away to the enemy.

Across the wire, the advancing tanks made fine targets against the white backdrop. The German 27th Infantry Division noted that 'ordinary wire entanglements are easily overcome by the tanks', however, 'high, dense and broad entanglements' were 'apt to get entangled with the tracks of the tanks.' Noting the effectiveness of armour piercing ammunition, the Germans documented how the 'greatest danger for the tanks is the ready inflammability of petrol and oil. Machine gun fire is capable of igniting them.' Artillery knocked out seven British tanks on 11 April 1916. Small trench guns, the Germans documented, 'should be kept in dug outs up to the actual moment of coming into action when they deliver fire at point-blank range.' Trench mortars, or Minenwerfer (mine thrower), 'are also suitable for anti-tank defence.' While the 'moral effect of tanks on the infantry' was significant, it was 'somewhat minimised in this division by the successful repulse of the tank attack'. The Germans now viewed the tank as only a limited threat, one easily dealt with by existing anti-tank tactics and weaponry. Britain, in the meantime, had suffered more than 150,000 casualties by the end of the Somme offensive – and for very little gain. The battlefield returned to deadlock.

(**Opposite, above**) The light 7.6cm Minenwerfer was originally designed for trench warfare and high angle fire. It was later converted into a mobile infantry gun capable of high angle and flat trajectory fire. Unteroffizier Petzold, German Infantry Regiment 27, wrote: '… every shot was impacting on those stinking boxes known as "tanks". Each time one of these objects went up in flames, the brave lads of the infantry cheered and exchanged ribald comments. "It must be warm for the crew in there!" Yes, our guns shot really well.' German intelligence later noted from combat reports that the 'impact of machine gun bullets upon the armour plating creates sparks within the interior which create the impression that the tank is on fire and greatly disquiets the driver and gunner. Tank rifles are intensely feared.'

(**Opposite, below**) In enemy hands. The Mark II male D26 (No. 799), under the command of 20-year-old Welshman Second Lieutenant Harold Davies, was knocked out while leading Australian troops into battle near Bullecourt on 11 April 1917. Davies was killed in the action with most of his crew managing to escape. Note the absence of the tail wheels and the use of 'spuds' or 'grousers', a bolt-on track extension on the track plates to assist movement across soft ground but with an unfortunate habit of becoming entangled with barbed wire. Fifty Mark II tanks – twenty-five males (with the 'long' naval barrel) and twenty-five females – were delivered from December 1916 to January 1917 by Foster & Co. and Metropolitan. The unarmoured Mark II tank retained the cumbersome steering characteristics of its predecessor, which required the orchestrated efforts of a driver and gear men to affect a gear change or significant change in direction.

– Vor Arras erbeutete Tanks –

Four German postcards of the oft-photographed Mark II male D26 (No. 799) following its capture by troops of Grenadier-Regiment 123. The loss of tanks at Arras was unfortunate, J.F.C. Fuller recorded, 'for the Germans discovered that their latest armour-piercing bullets would penetrate their sides and sponsons. This discovery led to a German order being published that all infantry should in future carry a certain number of these bullets.' German analysis and firing trails subsequently revealed that the MK II's armour was easily penetrated by armour-piercing 7.92mm S.m.K. (*Spitzgeschoss mit Kern* – '*Kern*' referring to an iron core) ammunition, a battlefield weakness exacerbated with the vehicles slow speed and poor cross-country mobility. Crucially, the armour of the Mark II (training) tanks had not undergone the final hardening process during manufacture.

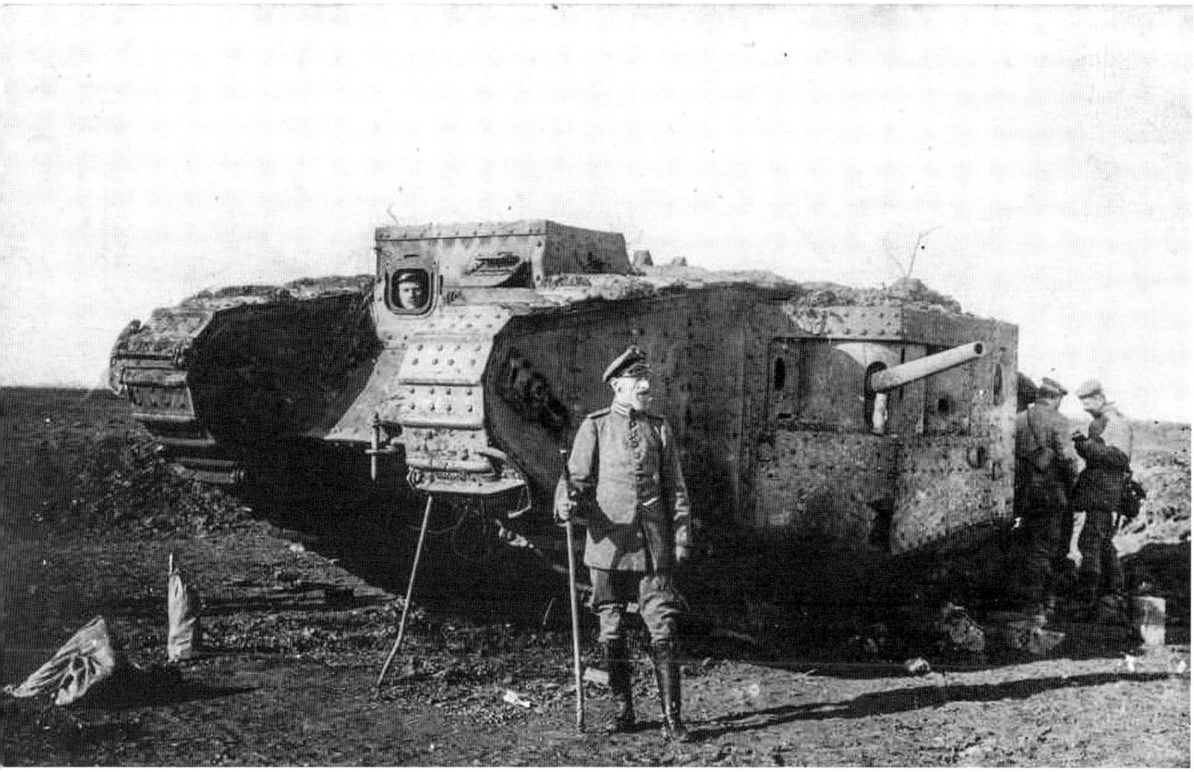

A later shot of No. 799, the right gun partially removed from the sponson. Leutnant Schabel, Grenadier-Regiment 123, was credited in *Die Württemberger im Weltkrieg* as the individual responsible for destroying the tank. In command of Machine Gun Company 3, Schabel fired 1,200 armour piercing rounds towards the tank at 150 yards. Three bullets penetrated the petrol tank, setting it alight. As the first tank to be destroyed behind German lines, it was something of a sensation with military 'visitors' keen to examine and study the machine.

Abandoned Mark II male at Bullecourt. Writing after the war, Field Marshal Erich Ludendorff reflected: 'As to the tanks, opinion was unanimous; they were not thought particularly dangerous. I purposely made use of the expression "tank-fright", but the officers from the front would not admit there was any such thing.'

Victor and victim across seasons. German soldiers pose beside a destroyed female Mark II tank. Swinton noted in February 1916 that enemy artillery posed the greatest threat to tanks: 'The only means by which we can at the earlier stages of an attack reduce the activity of the enemy's guns are by our own artillery fire or by dropping bombs on them from the air.'

French Tanks

Political rivalry in France led to the simultaneous development of two tanks: the Schneider CA1, under the auspices of Colonel Jean Estienne, 'father' of the French tank, and the Saint Chamond, designed by the *Société des Forges et Acieries de la Marine*. The latter vehicle, heavily armed with a 75mm gun and four machine guns, was slammed as the 'elephant on the legs of a gazelle' on account of its short, narrow tracks and excessive ground pressure. Schneider's CA1, based on a Holt tractor, resembled Britain's discarded prototype, Little Willie. It too possessed a host of design flaws including limited cross-country ability, poor mechanical reliability, insufficient ventilation and a propensity to catch fire given the exposed location of its forward fuel tanks.

British and French representatives met in Paris following the debut of French tanks in combat, one observer noting that the French party, including Estienne, 'generally seemed highly dissatisfied with the French tank'. J.F.C. Fuller noted privately that their 'big tanks are like kitchen ranges on tracks – quite useless.' Renault's revolutionary light tank, the FT, proved to be far more successful and, through an exchange, would have equipped British units had the war continued into 1919. The heavily armoured, multi-turreted, 69-ton Char 2C arrived too late to see action, entering service in

American troops beside a Schneider CA1, which first entered combat on 16 April 1917. The tank was armed with a limited traverse 75mm gun and two machine guns. The protruding steel spur on the front of the tank was intended to push through barbed wire obstacles.

The heavy Saint-Chamond (23 tons), another adaptation of the adaptation of the Holt tractor, was the second French tank to enter service. Plagued by inadequate vision and difficult for the crew to escape from, the recoil cylinder of the gun proved vulnerable to enemy fire.

War Illustrated reported on the Renault FT, a 6½-ton 'marvel of mobile speed' that could reach 4.3mph (7km/h).

'Mosquito' Tanks: Marvels of Mobile Speed

try of the new French " Mosquito " Tanks into the field of action. This small and mobile Tank, carrying a crew of two, played an important ·t in the brilliant counter-stroke on the Aisne by which General Foch forced the Germans to retire over the Marne on July 19th. It was in this fighting that the " Mosquitoes " were for the first time employed in considerable numbers.

1921. (Although Germany's A7V would possess a superior power to weight ratio to the French Schneider [14 tons] and Saint-Chamond [23 tons] tanks, it also shared many of the French machines' disadvantages.) Like the lowly opinion of captured British Mark II tanks, the disappointing debut of French models further coloured Germany's estimation of the tank.

Battle of Cambrai (20–30 November 1917)

Germany may have been less than impressed by the first Allied tanks, yet Entente observers conjectured when a hostile equivalent would make its appearance. 'A queer thing about the present fighting in the West is that nothing has been heard of German tanks taking part in it', an Australian editorial broached in early May 1917:

> Tanks would surely be useful for counter attacks, and the Germans must long ago [have] captured at least one specimen. As a matter of fact, they claim to have captured many, and also to have invented a tank of their own. This lack of German tanks is all the more surprising in view of the fact that some of the neutral nations are said to have already started to obtain tanks for their armies ... Perhaps Germany is still experimenting and means to come out by and by with a very superior article.

Still, as the paper added, 'the British tanks are also being improved, and are doing good service.' Tactical lessons from the fighting in April 1917 had indeed taught the value of concentrating tanks during an attack, the need for specialized supply and signal tanks, an understanding that early model tanks should not be deployed across wet, heavily shelled ground plus the necessity of counter-battery shellfire for security.

Britain's latest tank, the Mark IV, what some have described as the first main battle tank, featured in the November 1917 fighting at Cambrai – the first large-scale, successful use of armour. Nine tank battalions were assigned to the battle – a total of 432 fighting tanks plus supply, wireless, bridging and wire pulling tanks. Designed as a surprise raid, success would depend on surprise, the tanks' ability to negotiate the formidable Hindenburg line, and infantry following closely behind. Leutnant Hörold, 227th Reserve Infantry Regiment, recalled the moment he knew of the advancing armour: 'a grinding, roaring sound which was getting closer and a stink of petrol fumes was carried on the westerly wind. We knew what were on their way! – Tanks!' Significant gains were made on the first day, 20 November, a milestone in the history of warfare and a boon to the British public.

Cambrai, however, also revealed that the Mark IV tanks were simply too slow, allowing German troops to reposition or organise defences to obstruct their advance. Closer co-operation was likewise needed with infantry, artillery and aircraft to maximise any breakthrough. Like Arras, Cambrai demonstrated the danger artillery posed to armour, with German guns accounting for over one third of tank losses on the first day of fighting (65 out of 179 tanks lost). Leutnant Jakubasch, 213th Field Artillery Regiment, engaged oncoming tanks around Flesquières with field guns, later writing: 'In order to be able to engage them successfully we pulled the two serviceable guns out of their covered pits and moved them forward to where we could engage them with direct fire. With the manpower we had available it was not possible to push them up the steep slope to our front in order to obtain a perfect position. I ordered sights to be set at 700 metres and, with our third shot, we knocked out a tank. In short order we followed this with three more, then suddenly one of our guns failed mechanically. I then continued with my one remaining gun and dealt with four more tanks – the last of them at a range of 800 metres – so my total score was eight.'

Wehrmann Hohmann, 27th Infantry Regiment, witnessed a direct hit on a Mark IV: 'Within an instant it was enveloped in a large cloud of black smoke and the tank itself seemed to be ablaze. We suddenly saw the crew bale out and run away from the tank; naturally they did not get far under our fire.'

For General Erich Ludendorff, his infantry were the victors on this occasion. Writing after the war, he gave thought to the initial success of the 'very effective' British tanks and his army's response:

> In the fighting around Bourlon and Bourlon Wood our infantry had disposed of tanks at close quarters by multiple grenades [a stick grenade supplemented by multiple grenade heads]. Our artillery had shot them to pieces. Even the steel-cored bullets used by our machine guns had been good enough. The best weapons against tanks were good nerves, discipline, and intrepidity, which enabled many brave men to climb on them, or destroy them by short-range fire. Not until our infantry lost its discipline and fighting capacity did the employment of massed tanks combined with artificial smoke, produce a fatal effect on the course of events.

Stereograph of a Mark IV tank, favourably captioned: 'Our monster tanks break down the belts of barbed wire and completely surprise the Hun at Cambrai'. Production of the Mark IV tank began in March 1917, roughly two months behind schedule. The tank featured a shorter barrelled 6-pounder gun in a smaller, retractable sponson. The Lower muzzle velocity was not problematic since targets were mostly engaged over short distances. Solid shot rounds could penetrate 1.5 inches of armour at 500 yards. High Explosive ammunition was also carried.

(**Left**) *Wir schlagen sie – und zeichnen Kriegsanleihe!* ('We're beating them – and subscribing to the War Loan'). British tanks rendered in similar vein in a German appeal for war bonds. British tanks were dubbed 'devil's coaches'. Visual media – posters, postcards, photos and movies – played a leading role in mass communication during the conflict.

(**Opposite**) Knocked out tanks litter the Cambrai battlefield. Half of the 378 tanks were still operational on the second day of fighting. Aside from enemy fire, seventy-one succumbed to mechanical problems on the first day, forty-three were ditched. German artillery and infantry eventually ground down the British advance before a counteroffensive was launched on 28 November, recapturing most of the recently taken territory.

(**Below**) Designed as a mobile anti-aircraft platform, the truck-mounted 7.7cm Leichte Kraftwagengeschütze M1914, was used in an anti-tank role with deadly effect. The gunners of K-Flak-Geschütz 92 were credited with destroying seven tanks at. Cambrai. (NARA)

Engl. Tanks bei Cambrai
773

Engl. Tank aus der Schlacht bei Cambrai

Four images showing German soldiers as they inspect and pose by the Mark IV male B28 (No. 2080) *Black Arrow*, knocked out at Fontaine-Notre-Dame. Note the unditching beam. Although the The Mark IV incorporated several improvements over earlier models, it still lacked single driver control, which according to J.F.C. Fuller was 'exceedingly clumsy and often involved much loss of time and temper.'

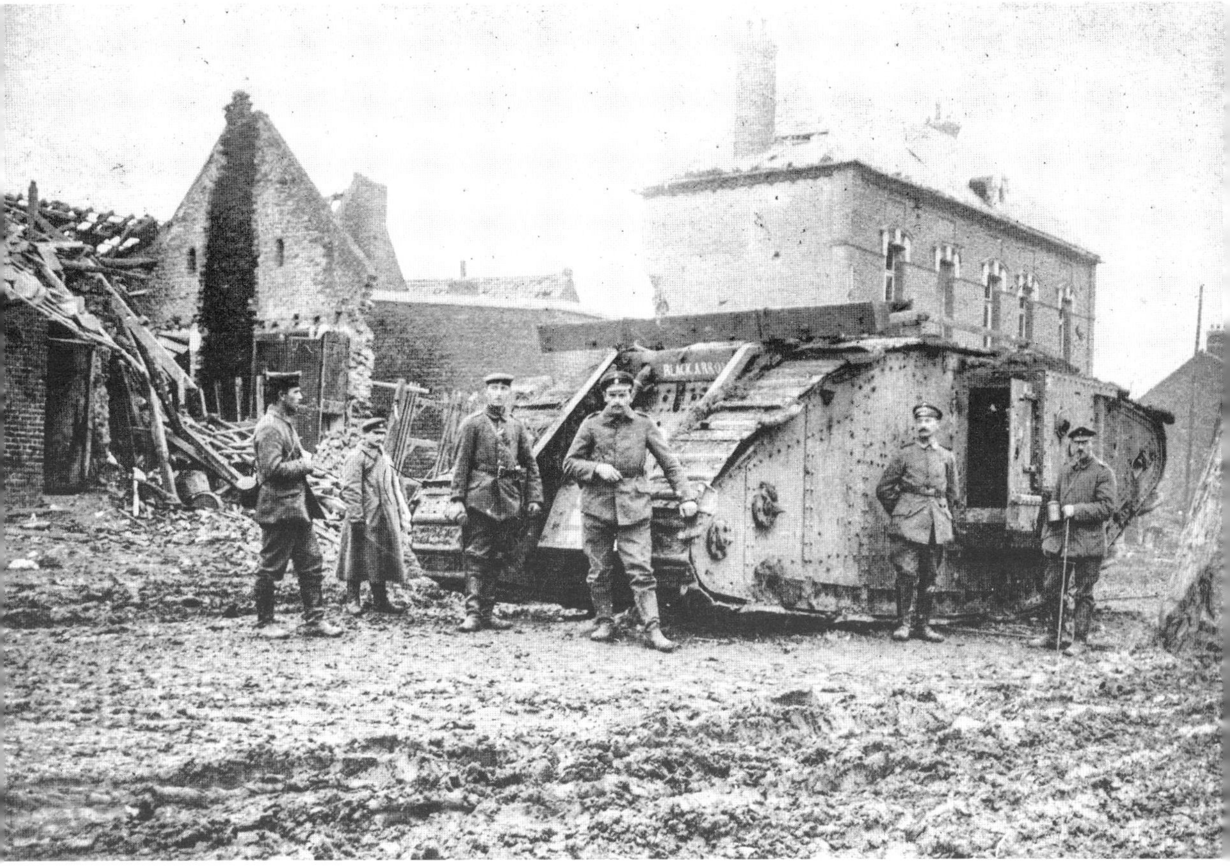

Newsreel footage of German troops inspecting knocked-out British armour – a mix of models: Mark IV male (top row); Mark II (middle row); Mark I or II (lower right).

Featuring a maximum of 14mm of armour, the Mark IV tank was most numerous of all British models with 476 deployed at Cambrai. 'There was horrible slaughter in Fontaine', Fuller later wrote, 'and I, who had spent weeks before the battle in thinking out its probabilities had never tackled the subject of village fighting. I could have kicked myself again and again for this lack of foresight, but it never occurred to me that our infantry commanders would thrust tanks into such places.' (National WWI Museum and Memorial)

A British tank commander in the battle of Bourlon Wood (southwest of Cambrai) recorded the dread of seeing a tank fall to enemy guns. He watched as one tank hesitated

> before it crossed the skyline, and our hearts went out to the driver in sympathy. He made his decision, and the tank, brown against the sky, was instantly encircled by little puffs of white smoke, shells from the guns on the reverse slope. The man was brave, for he followed the course of a trench along the crest of the hill. My companion uttered a low exclamation of horror. Flames were coming from the rear of the tank, but its guns continued to fire and the tank continued to move. Suddenly the driver must have realised what was happening. The tank swung towards home. It was too late. Flames burst from the roof and the tank stopped, but the sponson doors never opened and the crew never came out … When I left my post half an hour later the tank was still burning …

Curmudgeon II, tank C21 (No. 2061) was knocked out while attempting to clear enemy positions on Gonnelieu Spur on 20 November 1917. A British section commander whose tank had broken down recalled: 'In the sudden silence we could hear the thud of falling shells, and metal and earth striking the sides of the tank. Any moment it would be Kingdom Come. The atmosphere in the tank was foul. To the heat and smell of the engine were added cordite fumes and the fact that nine men had been confined in this small space for close on three hours. It was a trying moment.'

German troops pose by Mark IV male, 156 (No. 2363). The tank fought at Bourlon Wood, silencing a machine nest inside a Châteaux on the western side of the village before a punctured fuel tank forced the evacuation of the tank's eight crewmembers. Writing of the British armour, a Leutnant in Reserve Infantry Regiment 52 recalled: 'As the tanks drew closer, a lot of their fire passed very close to us, but they did not enjoy much success. However, it was really unpleasant when one of the tanks crossed and recrossed our line, engaging at point blank range with main armament and machine gun fire.'

Chaperon II, a Mark IV female, C51 (No. 2732), was lost south of Lateau Wood on 20 November 1917 after German artillery hits. The ace of spades insignia on the sponson refers to the 12th (Eastern) Division, a British infantry division to which it was allocated. A 1918 German intelligence report noted that 'since the hostile infantry usually follow up the tanks with very little élan, we have nearly always succeeded in separating the infantry from the tanks, thus compelling even those tanks which did not break through to retire.' (NAM)

Mark IV female C47, *Conqueror II* (No. 4651) was knocked out on 23 November 1917 after an AP round struck a petrol tank, engulfing the vehicle in flames. German troops had shadowed the tank for hours in a built-up area. The vehicle bore a painting of a German soldier surrendering – presumably to motivate others to follow.

Allied intelligence gained an insight into the reversal at Cambrai from interrogating a German officer and NCO: 'Rifle and artillery fire stopped the waves of infantry, so that the tanks which then advanced alone were easily attacked with hand grenades (concentrated charge) and small arms, with armour piercing bullets (*Spitzgeschoss mit Kern* or S.m.K. bullets); the artillery, of course, also took part in their destruction.' From these experiences, the German Army had (purportedly) drawn the following conclusions regarding the design and future use of tanks:

(1) Tanks must have greater speed (a large number of reports clearly indicate speeds averaging 8 kilometres per hour over broken ground).
(2) Tanks must be well armoured (the prisoners speak of protection against field artillery shells …)
(3) Tanks will go forward in a staggered formation, zigzagging frequently.
(4) Infantry protects the tanks not only in front but on the flanks also, the assault troops advancing on each side at intervals of 150–200 metres.

Notwithstanding losses, the press on both sides waxed lyrical about the success of British armour at Cambrai. A 'German Tribute To Tanks' appeared in the *New York*

Times on 29 November 1917, originally published in the *Kölnische Volkszeitung und Handels-Blatt* newspaper:

> What the Entente has so far not been able to accomplish by artillery fire – that is, to break through on our front – was achieved on the Cambrai front with tanks. In very great numbers (probably there were 400 of them) those monsters went on in advance of the hostile infantry, smashing down all obstacles, breaking through our lines and so cutting off our front line from all communication with the rear that it was subjected to fire from both the tanks and infantry. The approach of the tanks through the mist and the smoke of bursting shells was difficult to observe, and it can be said that the enemy succeeded in achieving a surprise attack.

Early breakthrough success at Cambrai similarly prompted *The Times* to conclude in December 1917 that it 'will doubtless give an impetus to the study of the "tank" problem by the enemy', though acknowledging 'they came into the field of war effort very late in the day indeed':

> They cannot now hope to manufacture the armoured leviathans as rapidly as the Allied nations, for they are inferior, not only in industrial power, but in material resources. But, even supposing that Hindenburg could put hundreds of tanks into the fighting line, it is evident that their value will depend very largely

Mark IV female *Ghurka* was knocked out on the fourth day of fighting in Bourlon Wood on 23 November 1917.

> on the aerial power he can command. Unless he can wrest the dominance of the air from the Allies he cannot surprise any portion of the western front with a massed formation of tanks, and it does not seem likely that his mailed monsters could exist long when the well-directed artillery fire of the Allies and the bomb attacks of the Allied aviators get into action.

Cambrai, however, not only encouraged OHL to hasten delivery of its first tank, then in development, but also to recover, recondition and deploy captured British Mark IV machines. Ironically, more turncoat tanks would see German service than their own design, the A7V-Sturmpanzerwagen. While Cambrai is today celebrated as the first large-scale armoured offensive, the attack proved costly with more than 80,000 men from both sides killed, wounded, or missing with little strategic effect on the Western Front. The fighting did, however, herald a change in armour and combined-arms tactics that would feature in the battles of 1918.

G21, *Grasshopper II*, and F6 (unluckily named) *Feu d'Artifice* (Firework) were knocked out on 23 November 1917. Generalleutnant Otto von Moser noted that 'numerous tanks were knocked out in front of Bourlon and in Bourlon Wood itself. Losses were high and the infantry is very worn down. It is fortunate that our artillery and airmen are gradually gaining the upper hand, otherwise the situation would be almost desperate.' Booty from knocked out tanks was prized. A Reserve Leutnant from Lehr Infantry Regiment recalled his men examining an enemy tank, 'both for rations and anything else that looked to be worth taking. We were able to capture several bars of chocolate, which we had long coveted, together with boxes of biscuits and a good compass.'

Mark IV female *Hot Spur II* (No. 4687) was hit by German artillery during a counter attack on the village of Doignes on 21 March 1918. In his 1920 book *Stahlgewittern* ('Storm of Steel'), Ernest Jünger wrote of inspecting 'shot-up tanks … I would have my company cluster round them to study methods of combating them, their tactics and their weak points – these ever-more commonly seen elephants of the technical war. They carried names and emblems and designs that were variously ironic, menacing or lucky; there was the clover leaf and the pig (for luck), and the white death's head … All of them were in a bad way.'

British Mark V* (pronounced 'star'), No. 9890, put out of action by German land mine and artillery fire on 29 September 1918. Note the semaphore paddles on the roof used for signalling other units. A Mark V tank was lost behind German lines on 23 July 1918, though local commanders failed to recognise the new model machine and salvage it for evaluation. (AWM E04941)

Chapter Four

Germany Tank Development

The introduction of the tank in September 1916, a weapon promising to restore manoeuvre warfare, encouraged German military authorities to likewise explore armoured vehicle development. Weeks later, a report from First Army Headquarters advised OHL that the novel vehicle was 'potentially noteworthy'. Adolf Wild von Hohenborn, Prussia's Minister of War, in reply, noted; 'Deserves serious attention despite some failures. We shall not be outwitted in any form!'. Barely a month after first encountering the Mark I, both OHL and the *Preußisches Kriegsministerium* (Prussian Ministry of War) were cognisant of meeting future threats. Accompanying drawings and descriptions of Britains tank in a note (dated 11 October 1916) from Ludendorff to the Ministry of War was a concurring view that,

> Without overestimating the appearance of these fighting vehicles, some results cannot be denied. An improved vehicle would be an effective weapon. I therefore see it as necessary that the construction of such a vehicle is started immediately ... As soon as a useful model is found, mass production of such vehicles ought to be started.

Von Hohenborn informed *Allgemene Kriegsdepartment 7 Abteilung Verkehrswesen* (General War Department, Section 7, [motorized] Transportation, or A7V) of the pressing need to produce a German equivalent of the 'tank'.

> Personal messages from the front encourage my opinion that we have a respectable opponent in the enemy's armoured vehicles, which can – improved and increased in numbers – become a serious disadvantage to us in the spring [of 1917]. The finalising of a German model is highly urgent.

An assortment of potential design options under development at the time by private industry included the Friedrich Wilhelm Göbel's farcical *Landpanzerkreuzer* ('armoured land cruiser'), a 550-ton behemoth, 118ft in length and armed with a central rotating turret and more than ten machine guns on each side, the Dür-Wagen (from Dürkopp), the Orion-Wagen, and the Treffas-Wagen (from Hansa-Lloyd, Bremen).

The prototype Orion-Wagen, seen during a demonstration of several prototype models on 14 May 1917. Underpowered with a 45hp engine and featuring a complex track design, this vehicle was slow and ineffective in crossing trenches. Still an order for fifty machines was placed with twenty-nine completed and sixteen eventually accepted into service where it performed poorly. A second prototype was completed in late 1917 minus the steering wheel and with the addition of a fully rotating turret failed to generate interest. A multi-turreted third prototype, resembling the Leichter Kampfpanzer remained on the drawing board.

Hansa-Lloyd's prototype Treffas-Wagen was completed on 1 February 1917. The impractical design featured two 3.3m (11ft) steel wheels, an armoured hull, and a rear wheel for steering.

THE TANKS.

GERMANY CLAIMS CREDIT

"Britain's Feeble Imitation."

(Reuter's Telegrams.)

LONDON, Saturday.

The "Lokal Anzeiger" claims that the "tanks" now being used by the British were invented by a German engineer years ago, and that the British production is only a feeble imitation. The story of the construction of monster Zeppelins able to carry five tons of bombs has reappeared, and it is stated in Petrograd that four of them are expected to be ready in October.

Ten examples were initially ordered before the Treffas-Wagen's disappointing trial results revealed a propensity for tipping over and becoming ditched.

Not to be outdone, Germany even claimed credit in September 1916 for inventing the tank, panning 'Britain's feeble imitation.'

Germany's most promising early design was Hugo Bremmer's prototype caterpillar tracked vehicle, produced at the Daimler-Motoren-Gesellschaft factory at Berlin-Marienfelde. Named after its inventor, the Bremer-Wagen (or Marienwagen), it was essentially a standard Daimler truck with tracks replacing wheels. It was unveiled before an audience at Neheim, Westphalia on 6 October 1916 – just days after the first report of Britain's tank – as the basis for an all-terrain vehicle. The War Ministry's decision to produce further experimental models, however, proved disastrous. The stopgap *Marienwagen I mit Panzeraufbau* (with a mock-up superstructure) was demonstrated to Field Marshal Paul von Hindenburg, his deputy, General Erich Ludendorff and members of the General Staff at Mainzer Sand on 11 March 1917. Saddled with an armoured superstructure, the underpowered armoured fighting vehicle was dogged by low ground clearance, a high centre of gravity and inadequate cross-country mobility. What could be called Germany's first tank was a cumbersome machine that failed to impress those present, Ludendorff in particular losing interest in further tank development. An order for the formation of Marienwagen units was rescinded on 3 April 1917, thus shifting the focus to a parallel project code-named A7V after the responsible War Ministry department.

(**Below**) Hugo Bremmer's Bremer-Wagen or Marienwagen, based on a remodelled Daimler chassis, was the basis for Germany's first armoured fighting vehicle. The transmission drove the rear set of tracks, sprung on semi-elliptic leaf springs. Similarly sprung, the front tracks were not driven and used only for steering.

(**Opposite, above**) More of an armoured personnel carrier than a tank, the cumbersome *Marienwagen I mit Panzeraufbau* was unarmed, although firing ports were provided in the box-like superstructure.

(**Below**) Following the failure of the Marienwagen I, Daimler produced a successful half-track design based on a Daimler Marienfelde ALZ 13 truck and Holt caterpillar system. A contract was awarded to produce 170 vehicles, though wartime exigencies saw only forty Marienwagen IIs were delivered before the November 1918 Armistice. This vehicle was one of a handful of machines given to the Latvian Army by the Allied Control Commission.

Interestingly, a semi-tracked version of the Marienwagen with the armoured hull from an Ehrhardt armoured car was concocted postwar to quell unrest during the Sparticist uprising. It foreshadowed the Wehrmacht's use of armoured half-tracks during the Second World War.

A mittlerer Schützenpanzer Sd.Kfz.251/1 (Ausf.A) in Berlin, 1940. This was Nazi Germany's most numerous half-track with over 15,0000 examples manufactured across twenty-two variants. (Bundesarchiv, Bild 1011-801-0664-37)

Tasked with monitoring enemy fighting vehicle development, Brigadier General John Charteris (head of intelligence at GHQ) expressed his concern to Major General George Macdonogh (director of military intelligence at the War Office) on 1 October 1916, requesting 'timely information'. Reports of enemy activity were soon at hand. One from Copenhagen (in December) stated that six 'machines resembling our tanks' were under construction in Essen.' A subsequent memo from Italy revealed that:

> the Germans are in possession of particulars [of] English tanks and are constructing [a] machine larger and more powerful type to take larger crew, more machine guns also quick firing guns. Framework being made in Berlin. Armour plate at Krupp's Works, motors at Chemnitz. They are not yet in service. Result[s] of trials not known.

Despite errors in geographical and industrial attribution, the report correctly revealed how several companies were collaborating on a tank project. Under pressure of time, in lieu of an open tender, a meeting convened on 30 October 1916, brought together the so-called 'A7V Committee' together with experts from some of Germany's leading firms, including Nationale Automobil-Gesellschaft (NAG), Daimler-Motoren-Gesellschaft (DMG), Dürkopp, Hansa-Lloyd Werke AG, Benz & Cie, and Büssing AG. Planning began for the design of a new tank, equivalent to the British Mark I, under the direction of engineer and automobile pioneer Joseph Vollmer, a senior engineer in the *Verkehrstechnische Prüfungs-kommission* (Motor Transport Inspection Service, or VPK). Specifications were issued for a vehicle with good cross-country performance; the ability to cross a 1.5m trench and climb a 1:10 gradient cross country; a road speed of 12km/h, 6km/h cross country; a weight of 30 tonnes; engine capacity of 80–100hp; forward and rear firing guns plus machine guns (with 6,000 rounds of ammunition) on each side; and the capacity to carry a reserve crew member. Curiously no mention was made of armour thickness, though this may have been due to concurrent testing of a new armour-piercing bullet.

Contracts were subsequently awarded, despite no finalised design, in November 1916 to sixteen companies including Dürkopp, Hansa-Lloyd, Apollo-Werke AG, and Daimler for engines; Alderwerke for differentials and gearboxes; Oberusel for radiators; Krupp and Dillinger Hüttenwerke for armour plate and Berlin-Anhaltische Maschinenbau Aktiengesellschaft (BAMAG) for machine tools. One of the A7V committee's first steps was to acquire and trial a Holt tractor from Austria. Payment was made to Holt for using its caterpillar design in the track system and an experienced Hungarian driver was brought to Berlin. The project became even more complicated upon OHL's request on 15 November for the chassis to operate as either a tank, or an all-terrain transport vehicle without armour and weapons – the Geländewagen or Überlandwagen ('overland vehicle'). To Vollmer's credit, plans for the A7V prototype were completed on 22 December 1916 based on a lengthened Holt chassis powered by twin Daimler 100hp engines.

Progress was swift. Daimler-Motoren-Gesellschaft (DMG) in Berlin-Marienfelde unveiled a mock-up of the hull on 16 January 1917. The vehicle s first demonstration followed at the company s proving ground on 30 April. It should be remembered that German engineers had independently pioneered their machine since the first British tank (D26/799) was captured only weeks earlier at Arras on 11 April.

After reviewing various design proposals, OHL decided on 14 May to form two A7V Abteilung, each of five tanks, plus supporting vehicles and personnel. Inferior proposals, such as the Treffas-Wagen, were abandoned, though approval was given for the manufacture of ten K-Wagen: five to be built by Waggonfabrik Wegmann and Co. in Kassel and another five by Riebe Kugellagerwerke in Berlin-Weissensee. Work on the new designes commenced despite tank production being accorded a low priority amid enthusiasm for new storm-trooper tactics.

Joseph Vollmer (13 February 1871–9 October 1955), the son of a locksmith, was a pioneering tank engineer who oversaw the design and production of Germany's first tanks – the A7V, K-Wagen, LK I and LK II.

Vollmer's A7V prototype in Spring 1917 showing commander and driver. The vehicle was designed to be operated by two opposite-facing drivers, sitting atop the two 4-cylinder, in-line, water cooled engines, for either forward or reverse operation. The steering in the centre of vehicle permitted observation in all directions.

The Überlandwagen or Geländewagen all-terrain supply carrier. Requested by OHL, the cross-country vehicle was based on the first A7V production chassis. Bearing Third Army registration, this vehicle (above) assisted in British tank salvage operations at Cambrai in the Second Army sector. Note the canopy over the driving position, wooden dropsides and tow hook. (NARA)

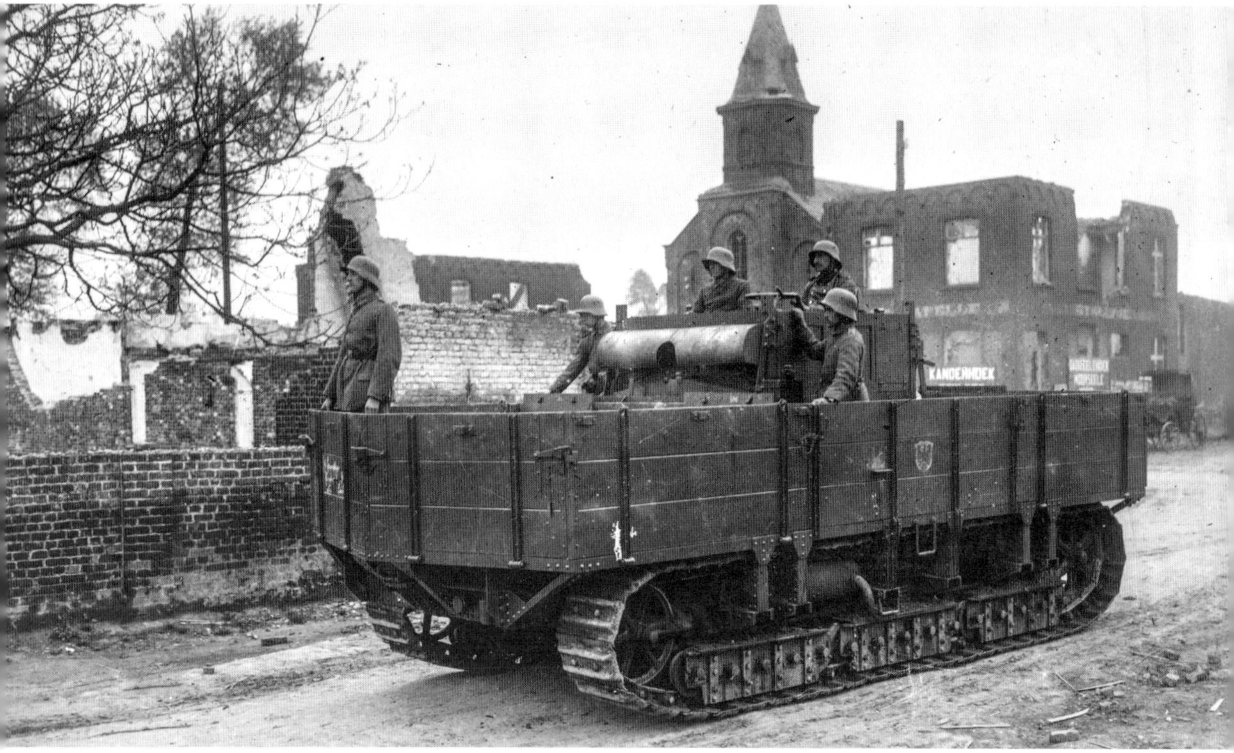

A7V Überlandwagen (minus canopy and cargo tarpaulin) originally captioned to be supplying ammunition to the front line at Ypres, 1918. With a crew of three, the vehicle could deliver 3–4 tons of cargo, though its cross-country mobility was compromised by the overhanging cargo bed and poor terrain handling. (NARA)

A mock-up of the A7V with wooden superstructure was tested in May 1917. Ten tons of ballast was carried to simulate the weight of the armour. Neither Ludendorff nor Hindenburg were present after the earlier Marienwagen debacle. The vehicle was later unveiled before the Kaiser on 19 June 1917. Assisted by a sophisticated transmission and twenty-four sprung rollers, the A7V performed well on paved and unpaved even surfaces. A boom with a spring-loaded roller was initially attached to the front of the tank to aid manoeuvrability across trench systems.

A7V-U

Cambrai gave fresh impetus to tank production with with OHL notifying the Ministry of War and the *Chef des Feldkraftfahrwesens* (Head of Field Motor Transport, or *Chefkraft*) that 'recent battles of the Second Army again showed the large moral and tactical impact of tanks in battle.' Elevated in resource priority for (iron and steel), a further ten A7V 'units of armour' were approved on 13 December 1917, the total number of vehicles capped at thirty-eight. Differences, however, arose between OHL and VPK regarding the allocation and use of the A7V chassis. Whereas VPK originally ordered 100 tanks, it now proposed building 200 tanks, only to have OHL finalise the production of 100 A7V chassis with only twenty produced as tanks, the remainder to be completed as unarmoured Überlandwagen. Due to production constraints and the stringent Hindenburg programme of August 1916 that called for the more efficient use of scarce resources, VPK approached the Ministry of War to expedite delivery of raw materials, even suggesting the official decoration of industrialists whose firms sped up production. Further difficulties arose from OHL pressuring A7V engineers to render the vehicle safe from shell fire on all sides. VPK responded with the veiled threat that increasing armour and reducing the number of weapons would

The A7V-U prototype featured 30mm of frontal armour, 20mm of side and roof armour. Powered by two Daimler 100hp engines, the vehicle had a maximum speed of 7mph (11kph) on roads and 3mph (5kph) cross country. A smaller version, the A7V-U2, was planned with smaller sponsons with a variant mounting only machine guns, though neither was produced. Development of the A7V-U ceased on 12 September, 1918. The prototype machine was transferred to the Berlin tank driving school and later scrapped.

run counter to one of the cardinal principles of army doctrine – *Wirkung geht vor Deckung* ('The effect of firepower outweighs protection'). Such an argument must be viewed in the context of the breaking the trench impasse, which in itself was a violation of German mobile tactical theory. OHL nevertheless stood firm with its small quota of tanks. It also ordered VPK to replicate the British rhomboid design, what became the A7V-U.

VPK's Sturmpanzerwagen A7V-U (A7V-*Umlaufendekette* or 'all round tracks') featured a rhomboidal-shaped hull on a standard A7V chassis (524). The A7V-U is seen here prior to installation of sponson, superstructure and armament. The sprung bogie suspension from A7V was retained with the tracks passing around the vehicle to emulate the superior cross-country superiority of British tanks. Note chassis 523 to the left.

Vollmer s 40-ton prototype was completed by Daimler-Benz in June 1918. Side sponsons mounted either 5.7cm or 7.7cm guns. The commander's cabin was larger than the A7V with the crew reduced to seven men. An order for twenty vehicles was placed in September before the project was abandoned. Nose-heavy with a high centre of gravity, the tank was plagued by manoeuvrability problems and poor performance. Note the chassis number.

K-Wagen

Chefkraft pursued development of another vehicle – a super-heavy breakthrough tank for offensive use on the Western Front. The colossal machine was designed to be broken down into three sections for rail transport before reassembly behind the frontline using specially built truck-mounted cranes. A draft design from Joseph Vollmer and Hauptman Weger was approved three months after an order was placed on 31 March 1917, despite Vollmer slamming it as impractical. The *Großkampfwagen* (heavy fighting vehicle) or G.K-Wagen was later known as the K-Wagen.

K-Wagen specifications: length, 12.7 metres; height, 3 metres; and width, 6 metres. Powered by twin 6-cylinder 60hp engines, delivering 1,300hp, the 120-ton colossus had a theoretical top speed of 7.5km/h (4.7mph). A true 'landship', it featured submarine clutches and ship engines. The two prototypes under construction were scrapped with US intelligence in Berlin later documenting that one completed tank was destroyed in November 1918, 'by the German workmen, who feared its use in internal troubles about the time of the revolution.'

The K-Wagen, seen here on the cover (centre) of Ernst Volckhiem's 1937 *Die deutschen Kampfwagen im Weltkriege* ('*The German Tank in the World War*'), was intended to carry four 7.7cm guns and six or seven machine guns. Plans to mount two flamethrowers were abandoned. The twenty-seven-man crew included commander, artillery officer, two drivers, two machinists, twelve gunners, eight machine gunners and a signaller.

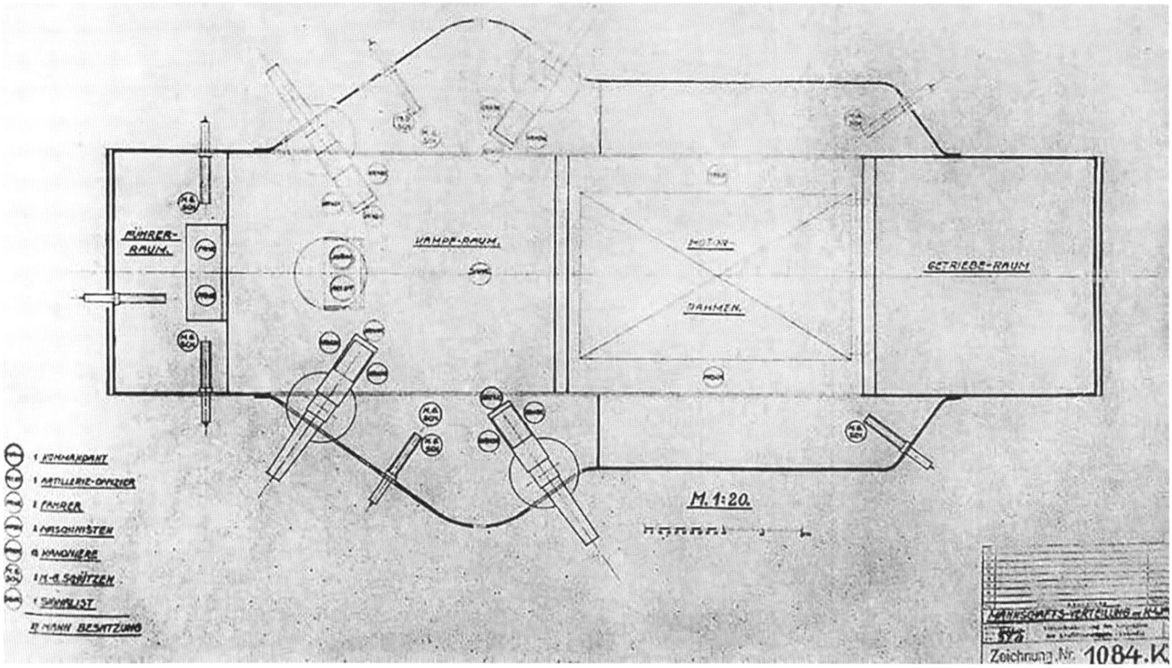

K-Wagen schematic.

Conjecture exists whether Hitler was aware of the K-Wagen. As in 1918, fanciful super-heavy designs appeared in Germany during the Second World War. Efforts to innovate gave rise to the 188-tonne Panzerkampfwagen VIII Maus and Krupp's proposed Landkreuzer P. 1000 Ratte ('Rat)', a 1,000-ton landship equipped with seven turrets. In this photograph, Hitler inspects a wooden mock-up of the Maus. The subsequent super heavy prototype was armed with a 12.8cm and 7.5cm gun and protected by 220mm of frontal armour.

Leichter Kampfpanzer

In further parallel development, Vollmer turned his attention to developing light tanks in May 1917. His idea was to marry a redundant car chassis with tracks, thin armour and machine guns. Lacking the protection of the A7V, the *Leichter Kampfpanzer* ('light battle tank'), as it was called, would nevertheless exceed it in speed, agility and ease of production. Although OHL rejected Joseph Vollmer's first light tank, the LK I, in early 1918 as inadequately armoured, *Chefkraft* requested a second, more heavily armoured model. Vollmer managed to complete two examples of his three-man LK II tank plus parts before the Armistice. Later imported by the Swedish government, under the façade of purchasing boiler plates and tractor parts, ten LK II tanks were assembled as the Stridsvagn m/21 (Strv m/21). Originally armed with a single 6.5 mm Schwarzlose machine gun, five vehicles were later rebuilt in 1929 as the Strv fm/21-29 variant, featuring a more powerful Scania-Vabis engine and a 37mm gun or twin machine guns. Vollmer's tanks served with the Swedish army until 1938 when they were replaced by the Czech CKD AH-IV tankette, known in Swedish service as the Strv m/37.

Vollmer's Leichter Kampfpanzer 1 (LK 1) utilised an existing Daimler car chassis with drive sprockets substituted for the rear wheels. Weighing 7 tons, the machine measured 18ft (5.5m) long, 6ft 6in (2m) wide and 8ft 3in (2.5m) in height. Protected by up to 8mm of armour, it carried a single machine gun in the revolving turret plus a second covering the rear. The front-mounted 40hp engine delivered a top speed of 12mph (20km/h).

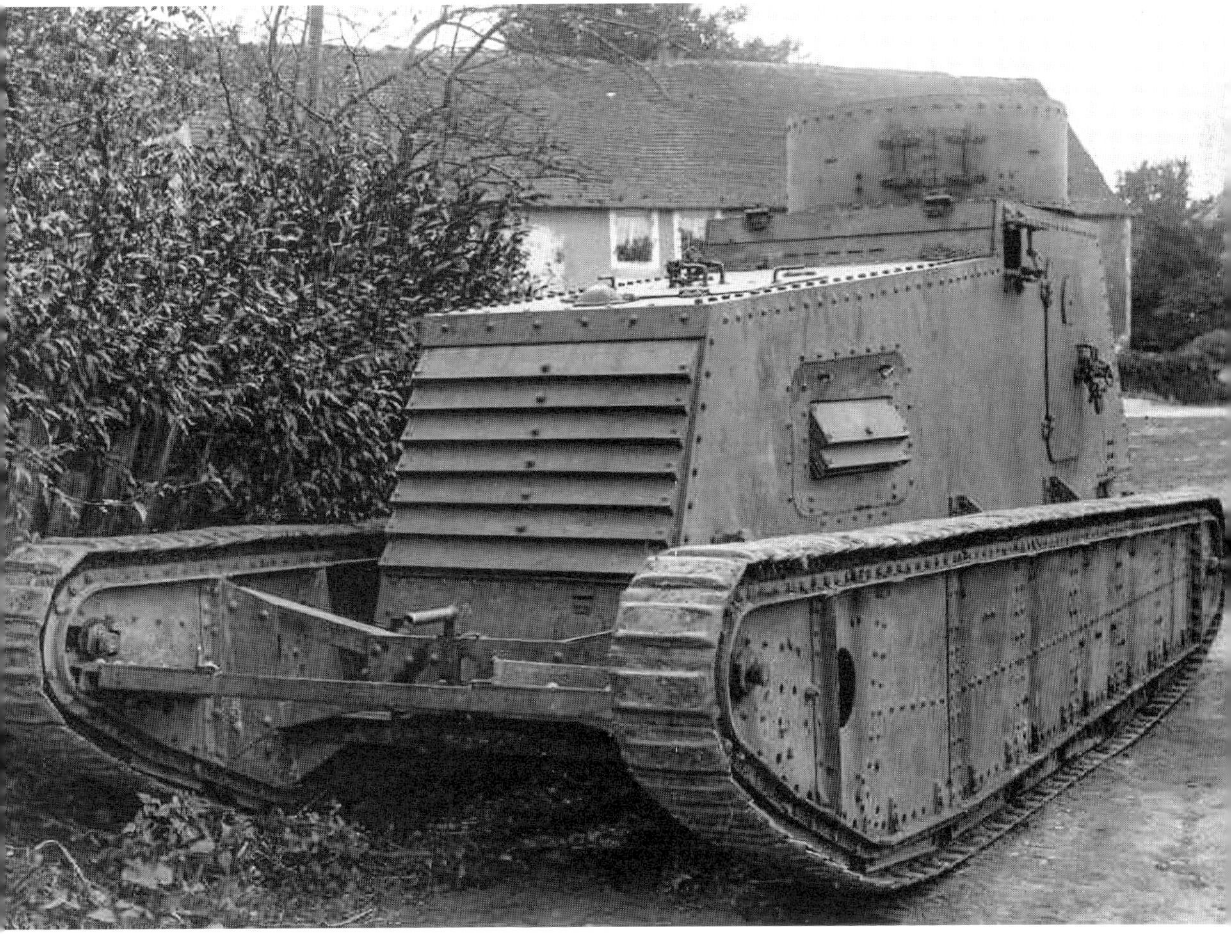

Similar in size to the LK I, the Leichter Kampfwagen II was protected by up to 14mm of armour with a larger Daimler-Benz 60hp engine giving a speed of 7mph (12km/h) during trials. It carried a Krupp 37mm gun.

Swedish Army Stridsvagn m/21 (Strv m/21). After driving one of the tanks in Sweden in 1929, Heinz Guderian (later proponent of the Third Reich's Panzer divisions), recalled: 'With their armour plating, their tracks, their guns and their machine guns, they succeeded in carrying their crews, alive and capable of fighting through artillery barrages and wire entanglements, over trench systems and shell craters, into the centre of German lines. The power of the offensive had come back into its own.'

Germany's LK II soldiered on as the reconditioned Stridsvagn fm/21-29 until a year before the war. By request, an example was purportedly sent to Germany in 1938 as a museum piece, only to disappear during the conflict.

The Swedes replaced the original 55hp Benz engine with a Scania-Vabis 85hp engine.

Vollmer moved to Czechoslovakia after the war. His design for a wheel-cum-track artillery tractor based on a Hanomag Z WD-50 became the KH-50 (KH an abbreviation of *Kolohousenka* from the Czech words *kolo* and *housenka* meaning 'wheel' and 'caterpillar'). The later KH-60 was abandoned in favour of the British Carden-Loyd tankette and the entire *Kolohousenka* programme was shut down after the unsuccessful KH-70 model of 1929.

A7V Production

The first ten A7V hulls, ordered in January 1917, were followed by a second batch in May 1917. Chassis numbered 501, 505, 506, 507 and 540 received armour plate provided by Röchling; chassis numbers 503, 504, 541, 542 and 543 received Krupp armour (540 was an anomaly, modified with Krupp armour in April 1918). Both companies were familiar with manufacturing armour for ship hulls. Whereas the Röchling plates were made to specification, the Krupp armour required cutting and straightening, resulting in a multi-panelled hull easily distinguished from its Röchling counterpart. It is understood that armour plate for the second batch of ten vehicles (chassis numbers 525, 526, 527, 528, 529, 560, 561, 562, 563, 564) was also supplied by Röchling. Field and factory modifications, including an extended exhaust pipe, rounding of the front and side mudflaps, extra cupola armour, elimination of a retractable signalling light plus later repairs, would see a fleet of externally distinct vehicles.

Original plans for arming the A7V with a 2cm Becker TUF (*Tank und Fleiger*) automatic cannon were dropped in favour of the British male/female configuration. Various calibre guns were considered, including a 7.7cm Feldkanone 96 neuer Art (7.7cm FK 96 n.A.), before Vollmer selected the 5.7cm Maxim-Nordenfelt quick-firing cannon, a weapon capable of penetrating 15mm of armour at 2,000 metres or 20mm of armour at 1,000 metres. In addition to six MG08 machine guns with 3,000 rounds, each tank carried a light MG 08/15 machine, four Gewehr 98 (M98) bolt-action rifles and twenty grenades.

The first production A7V, 501, undergoing trials at the Daimler works in Berlin-Marienfelde during November-December 1917. The vehicle, the only female A7V armed solely with machine guns to see action, was delivered in late October 1917, some twelve months after development began. The vehicle was subsequently rearmed with a 5.7cm cannon.

A mix of four A7V (the closest 501) and two A7V-Überlandwagen.

A7V cross section Note the sprung suspension and separate engine and fighting compartments.

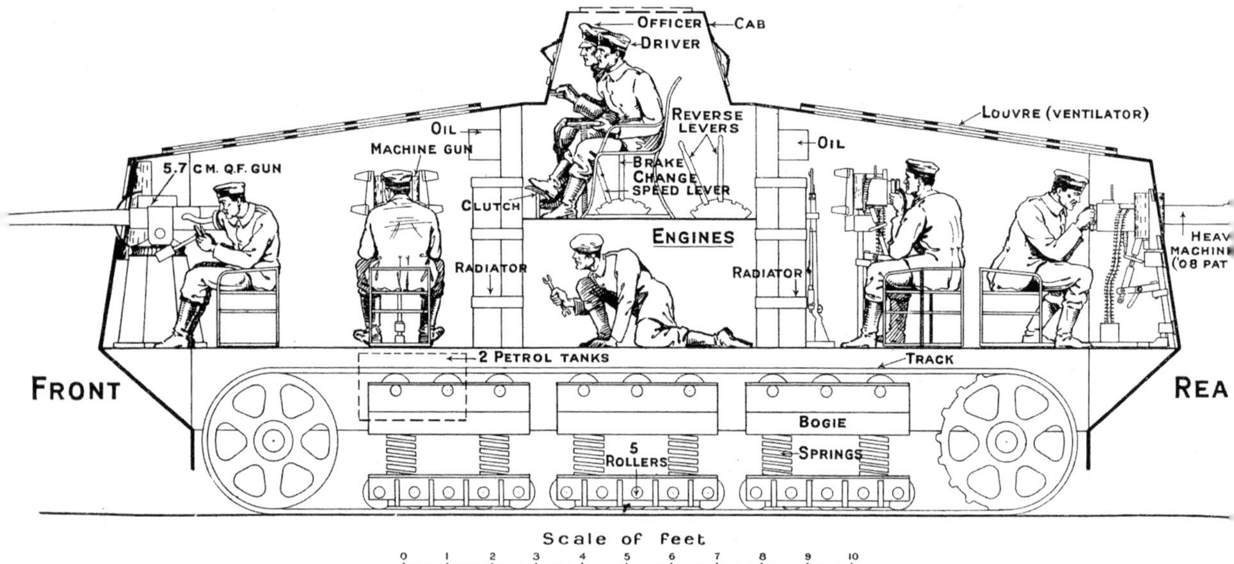

A7V Technical Data

Manufacturer	Daimler-Motoren-Gesellschaft, Marienfelde, Berlin.
Crew	18 men, typically an officer (Leutnant or Oberleutnant), driver, driver/mechanic, 12 machine gunners (6 gunners, 6 loaders) and 2 cannon gunners (gunner, loader), though up to 22 men were sometimes carried.
Engine	Two DMG 4-cylinder in-line engines 100hp (74kW) each at 800–900rpm, giving a power to weight ratio of 5.1kW/ton (6.8hp/ton)
Fuel consumption	Approximately 7.5 litres/km (road) or 16 litres/km (off-road)
Starter	electric starter/crank starter operated by three people
Fuel capacity	500 litres in 2 × 250 litre tanks
Operational range	60–70km (road) / 30–35km (off-road)
Speed	16km/h (road) / 4–8km/h (off-road)
Length / width / height	7.35m / 3.06m / 3.35m
Suspension	Holt track, 24 × vertical sprung wheels
Track width	2.115m
Ground clearance	20cm
Trench crossing capability	2 metres
Wading depth	80cm
Climbing ability	40cm / 25°
Total weight	30 tons
Armour	front 30mm, sides 15mm, roof 6mm, bottom front 10mm
Armament	1 Cockerill-Nordenfelt rapid-fire 5.7cm L/26.3 cannon; 6 × MG-08 machine guns.
Ammunition	180 × 5.7cm shells (a mix of 90 canister, 36 HE and 54 anti-tank rounds) later increased to 300; up to 18,000 machine gun rounds
Manufacturing costs	250,000 Marks
Communication	Light signalling device for fire orders; carrier pigeons for message relay.

Ernst Volckheim discussed the merits of the of the A7V In a postwar precis:

> In contrast to the layout of the enemy tanks the tracks of the A7V-Sturmpanzerwagen were protected by armour plates. The fact that each track was powered by one engine resulted in a better steering performance. Due to the thicker armour, vulnerability to enemy fire was lower. On the other hand, the mobility of the A7V in rugged terrain, under constant artillery fire, was significantly worse. Trenches and shell craters caused serious problems. The strong armour protection offered sufficient protection against infantry fire. The heavy German tank was even safe against hits from armour-piercing rounds …

Accurately reporting on enemy developments, London's *Times* revealed in December 1917 that 'the Germans are now experimenting with an armoured tank moving on caterpillars and armed with one 3-inch gun and two machine guns. It is fitted with a sort of beak forward to assist it in crossing trenches, and a small conning tower for observation purposes projects from the roof. The armour comes down well over the lower parts of the machine, so as to protect caterpillars, which are said to be completely hidden by armour.'

'Each track', a 1923 article in the US *Journal of the Army Ordnance Association* stated, 'has three roller trucks with five rollers each, the centre and outer rollers having a spur flange. Tie rods prevent the roller trucks from spreading apart on shifting position, while the upper part of the track is carried on support rollers. Because of uneven wear each track is fitted with an adjustable track take-up. With the tank steeply inclined, sidewise, the flanged track rollers engage in the double track rails, which in turn, reinforce the track plates laterally and prevent the rollers from siding up off the track shoe and thus prevent them from jumping the track.'

Close-up of 504 showing the driver's position (the commander seated on the left) and hinged central cupola panels. After examining a captured vehicle, an Allied intelligence report noted: 'Drive – one man control, each engine drives one track. There are two clutches, one change speed lever, two brake levers and two reverse levers, three speeds forward and three reverse, each track being driven independently. The tank is steered by turning the steering wheel in the direction required, this throttles down the engine on the required side. For sharp turns, if the turn should be to the right, clutch is disengaged, and the right-hand track brake is applied. There is an arrangement in the gear case by which one track can be put into forward and the other in reverse, but it is very doubtful if this would be required for steering.' (NARA)

A Reuters cable in January 1918 announced:

The news [of German-built tanks] causes no surprise; indeed, the surprise, if any, is that the enemy should have been so long in copying the example of the Allies, it being now well over a year since the travelling fortress, which quickly became known as the 'tank', made its first appearance, to the holy fear of the Hun soldiers, who had to face the onslaught of the new monster. It is hardly likely, however, that the news of the enemy having now a 'tank' on the way will disturb the peace of mind of either the French or British commanders-in-chief, for tanks

Unfortunate proof of the driver's blind spot ahead of the vehicle and unintended consequences. Allied examiners found that 'observation is exceptionally bad. Neither driver nor [commanding] officer can see the ground within 10 yards of the front of the tank. The gun and machine guns can be traversed on a point about 5 yards away from the tank.' This A7V, 562, was issued to Abteilung 1 on 2 April 1918. During an attack with 541 in an area south of Roye, Somme, on 9 June 1918, it was abandoned by its crew after plunging down a steep slope. Coming to rest on a French battalion command post, the startled occupants surrendered. Salvaged and repaired, the machine was transferred to Abteilung 2 as a replacement for *Nixe II*, 529, and named *Herkules*.

are rather instruments of attack than defence, and are consequently not likely to render such service to the Huns as they have done to the Allies. In any case we have more than a year's start over the enemy, not only in the construction, but also in the use of these machines, an advance which should enable us to more than maintain our supremacy in the 'tank' world.

A7V Variants

Of the A7V 100 chassis eventually produced, twenty-two were used to build two prototype and twenty production tanks. Another chassis became the A7V-U prototype, three were used for a Flakpanzer variant and two were deployed as a

Funkpanzer (radio tank) model. Besides the (aforementioned) Überlandwagen, other A7V variants included the A7V-*Schützengrabenbagger* (trench digger) and *Artillerie-zugmaschine* (a heavy artillery tractor). Other proposals that never left the drawing board included an observation or command tank and recovery vehicle.

The A7V Überlandwagen, hindered by the same mobility issues as the A7V, was also constrained by limited fuel availability. In Addition, the German General Staff held that caterpillar tracked vehicles were 'more suitable as armoured ammunition carriers than as potential armoured and mobile field batteries or nests of machine guns.' Note the swastika emblem, predating Nazi use, denoting *Armee-Kraftwagen-Kolonne (Raupe)* 1111 (AKK(R)1111) tracked transport column, the first Überlandwagen unit formed and dispatched to northern France in late 1917.

Three A7V Flakpanzer were built by Krupp in Essen to provide a mobile antiaircraft defense platform. With a central engine bay (like the Überlandwagen), the vehicle carried two captured Russian Model 1902 76.2mm guns on forward and rear platforms. Since Germany did not use guns of this calibre, specially adapted shells were manufactured since the actual gun barrels were too brittle to be rebored.

A single experimental A7V-Schützengrabenbagger was built by Lübecker Maschinenbaugesellschaft (LMG). The machine featured a shortened chassis with an excavator that could dig to 2.5m and dispose of earth via dual conveyor belts. The absence of armour would presumably jeopardize operations in combat situations.

Chapter Five

A7V Sturmpanzerwagen at War

The Sturmpanzerwagen A7V was the sole operational German-built tank of the war. Three A7V *Sturm-Panzerkampfwagen-Abteilungen* (assault armoured vehicle detachments) of five tanks (plus five in reserve) were created: Abteilung 1 on 5 January, Abteilung 2 on 22 March, and Abteilung 3 on 28 March 1918. Each Abteilung comprised seven officers, 171 NCOs and other ranks, plus four trucks, two cars and a motorcycle. Ernst Volckheim, A7V commander and future armoured warfare theorist, recalled how volunteers initially filled the ranks: 'The reason for this interest may be seen in the novelty of the weapon, the longer recreation phases between operations, the chance for promotion or decoration and, not least, in the good rations.' These men were drawn from traditional army branches – infantry for machine gunners, artillerymen for the 5.7cm guns and Kraftfahrtruppen (motor troops) for drivers.

After receiving its first A7Vs at Berlin-Marienfelde, Abteilung I began six weeks of tactical training in Sedan, France, site of the *Führer und Generalstabskurs* (Leaders and General Staff course). Showcased before Prince Eitel Friedrich of Prussia and General Max von Boehn on 14 January, Ludendorff and instructors watched a further demonstration on 25 February. Less than impressed, Ludendorff wrote: 'the impression was not a good one.' Criticism levelled at the A7V deemed it unsuitable for forthcoming battlefield operations. To help remedy the situation, the detachment was ordered to join the Sturmbataillon 5 (Rohr) – Hauptman Willy Rohr's elite assault battalion at Doncourt, near Beuveille. Part of the greenhorn A7V crews' training entailed removing all machine guns and joining accompanying infantry should their vehicle become immobilized. With drivers honing skills, tank crews became more adept at working with infantry. Rohr saw the tank's potential provided they were used on suitable terrain. At the same time British intelligence was digesting reports of German tanks allegedly in production from a variety of sources including agents, prisoners and deserters. Piecing together their adversary's progress, it was thought that up to 400 tanks were then under construction, a grossly inflated figure possibly sown by Berlin as part of pre-offensive deception.

A7Vs move through a French village.

As the first German tanks neared operational readiness, Ludendorff issued a handbook in January 1918 for the 'Deployment of Armoured Vehicle Assault Units'. It outlined the proposed role of the tank in:

> … offensive action, to support the advance of the infantry through
> (a) rolling over and destroying enemy obstacles,
> (b) the suppression of enemy troops, in particular those occupying bases and machine gun nests,
> (c) the repulsion of enemy counterstrikes.

Similar to stormtroopers, the tanks would not attack the enemy's strongest points, but instead drive through a weakly defended area, exploiting surprise, and clearing the way for an infantry breakthrough. It was emphasized that infantry were vital to the success of an armoured attack with close contact always needed. A tank could achieve a tactical breakthrough, infantry could hold territory gained.

A7V crewmen were supplied with padded brown leather helmets, asbestos overalls and a protective chain mail face mask with shutters over the eyes (centre). In practice, most crew members wore their standard service uniform.

An A7V trio advance toward German infantry positions during a training exercise. The German army manual *Merkblatt für das Verhalten der Infanterie beim Zusammenwirken mit Panzerwagen* (Notes on the Conduct of Infantry when Co-operating with Tanks) issued on 19 May 1918, taught: 'On longer distances the speed of the tanks is not adequate to keep up with the infantry. In such cases the infantry must not be hold up by the temporary falling back of the tanks but must fulfill its tasks as fast as possible regardless of the tanks' advance.' (AWM H13451)

A German flame thrower crew train their weapon towards an advancing A7V. 'The Kampfwagen were an assault weapon', Ernst Volckheim wrote after the war, 'designed to help the infantry. Their purpose was like the *Infanterie-Begleit-Batterien* [infantry support batteries] Along with the infantry Stoßtrupp they were to engage enemy strong-points, machine gun nests and other points of resistance. They were to destroy obstacles and break resistance as part of the spearhead to facilitate the easier progress of the following waves of infantry. To achieve this, a coordinated progression with the assault troops was needed.' (AWM H13456)

A A7V trio comprising 543 (foreground), 505 and 503 from *Abteilung* 2 in joint training with Bavarian Assault Battalion 15 near Saarburg. The single iron cross emblem on the hull side was synonymous with *Abteilung* 3. (NARA)

Propaganda image of 503 during training exercises on 1 October 1918. Delivered to *Abteilung* 3 in early April 1918 and named *Faust*, the tank's later monikers included *Kronprinz Wilhelm*, *Wilhelm* and *Heiland*. Regarding the A7V's armament, the US Tank Corps noted: 'the chief feature of this type would appear to be that the light gun, and the machine guns also, is mounted on the top of the tank. Thus, there is less danger of the tank being out of action when coming over the brow of a hill, before its guns can open fire.' (Bundesarchiv, Bild 146-1971-092-24)

A7V 563, *Wotan*. Judging the A7V, J.F.C. Fuller wrote: 'The chief characteristics of this [German] tank were its good speed on smooth ground, on which it could attain some eight mph; its inability to cross almost any type of trench or shelled ground on account of its shape. In weight it was about 40 tons, it carried very thick armour especially in front, capable of withstanding AP bullets at close range and field gun shells, not firing AP ammunition, at long; it was, however, very vulnerable to the splash of ordinary bullets on account of the crevices and joints in its armour. The most interesting feature of this otherwise indifferent machine was that its tracks were provided with heavy sprung bogies. The use of sprung tracks in so heavy a tank was the only progressive step shown in the German effort at tank production.'

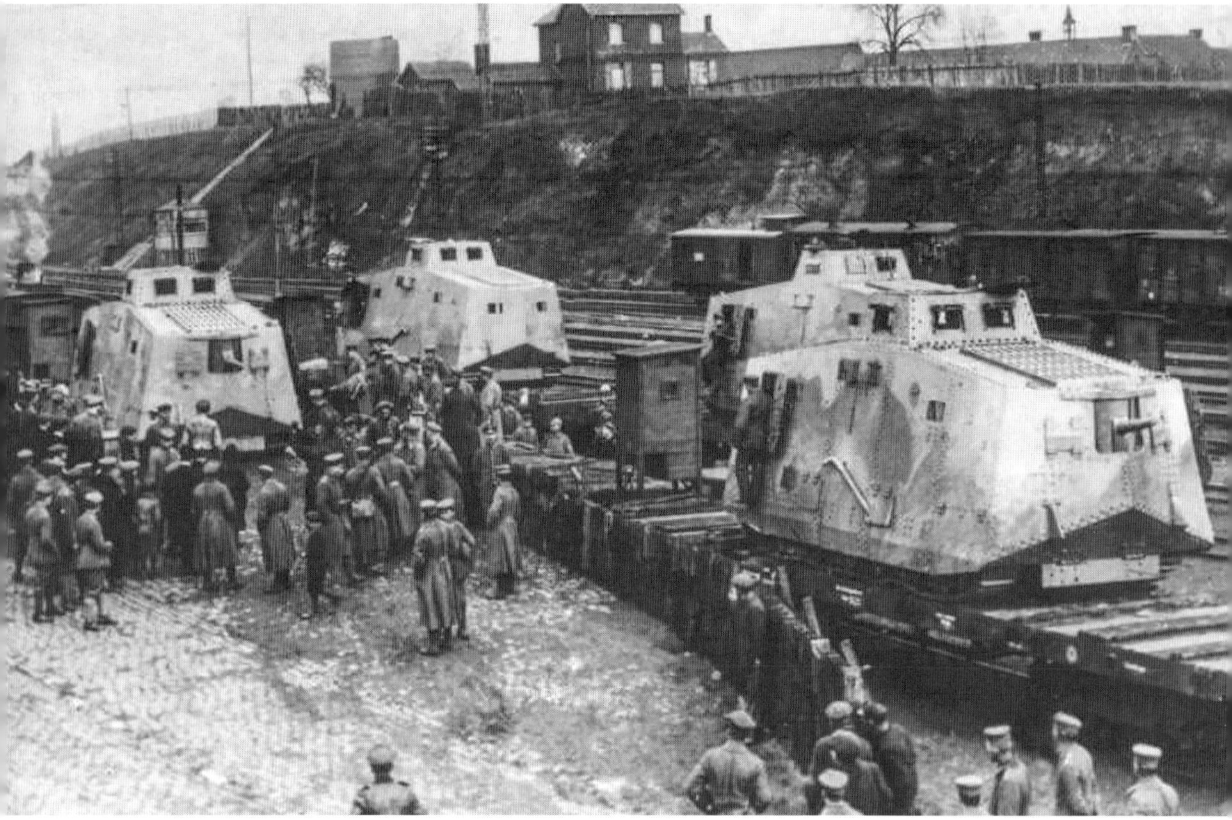

Newly arrived A7Vs at Monceau-sur-Sambre, a suburb of the Belgium town of Charleroi where the *Bayerische Armee-Kraftwagen-Park* 20 (Bavarian Army Motor Vehicle Park 20, or BAKP 20) workshops were located.

A7V Combat Debut at St Quentin

After three years of mostly defensive warfare, Ludendorff launched *Unternehmen Michael* on 21 March 1918. The ambitious spring offensive, designed to win the war, included the small-scale use of tanks. Ten tanks – five turncoat Mark IVs (Abteilung 11), and five Abteilung 1 A7Vs (501, 502, 505, 506, and 507) – were deployed (respectively) to the south and east of St Quentin. Gaps soon appeared in the ranks of the A7V Abteilung, beginning with 502, which succumbed to mechanical problems on the approach march. Fog, barbed wire and obstacles stymied the progress of the three remaining machines; 505 was entrapped in barbed wire. The driver of 506 recalled enemy artillery opening up: 'heavy calibre English ordnance tore into our positions with answering fire. Our surroundings are a milky grey colour; the air is heavy with fog, powder smoke poison gas … the landscape cloaked in invisibility.' (Volckheim later wrote that 'a light fog which permits vision to about 1,000 yards greatly assists the attacking tanks. It permits their unseen approach to within a short distance of the enemy and thus favours surprise.)

The armoured advance continued late morning once the mist lifted, though overheating and transmission problems halted 507. 'The heat has become unbearable',

German reserves advance through St Quentin. (AWM A03118)

A7V 506's driver detailed, 'The 200hp engines [*sic*] have been running uninterrupted now since 4.14 this morning.' The remaining A7V pair (501, 506) worked well with Infantry Division 36 troops, reaching the enemy trenches and causing panic. British troops in shock bolted from their positions. The two running tanks next advanced on a strongly defended French farmhouse and a position later described as a fortified quarry, bristling with machine guns and mortars. With 501 training its weapons on the British machine gunners, 506 fired grapeshot (or case shot) into the quarry from a distance. Moving forward, German storm troops captured six officers and 150 men from the London Rifles. A further enemy stronghold, referred to as the 'Entente Position' was taken with crew from 501 adopting the rehearsed infantry assault role and (purportedly) leaving their vehicle with portable flame throwers to clear the trenches.

Britain's *Daily Mail* later reported a wounded British officer's opinion that 'had it not been for a heavy blanket of mist and smoke that covered No Man's Land in the early hours of 21 March the attack, colossal as it undoubtedly was, would have been smashed at the jump. As it is, we simply have withdrawn to where we can get a better chance of killing them without being annihilated by their furious barrage. It will be our turn in a few days.' In another soldier's words, the A7V 'looked larger than ours, but were obviously working on the same principle. They moved slowly down a hillside and appeared to be bristling with guns and appliances for cutting wire.'

Newsreel footage of A7V 525, *Siegfried*. The intertitle reads: 'The most successful tanks *Gretchen* and *Siegfried* return from battle.

Siegfried

(**Below**) Newsreel footage of 501, *Gretchen*.

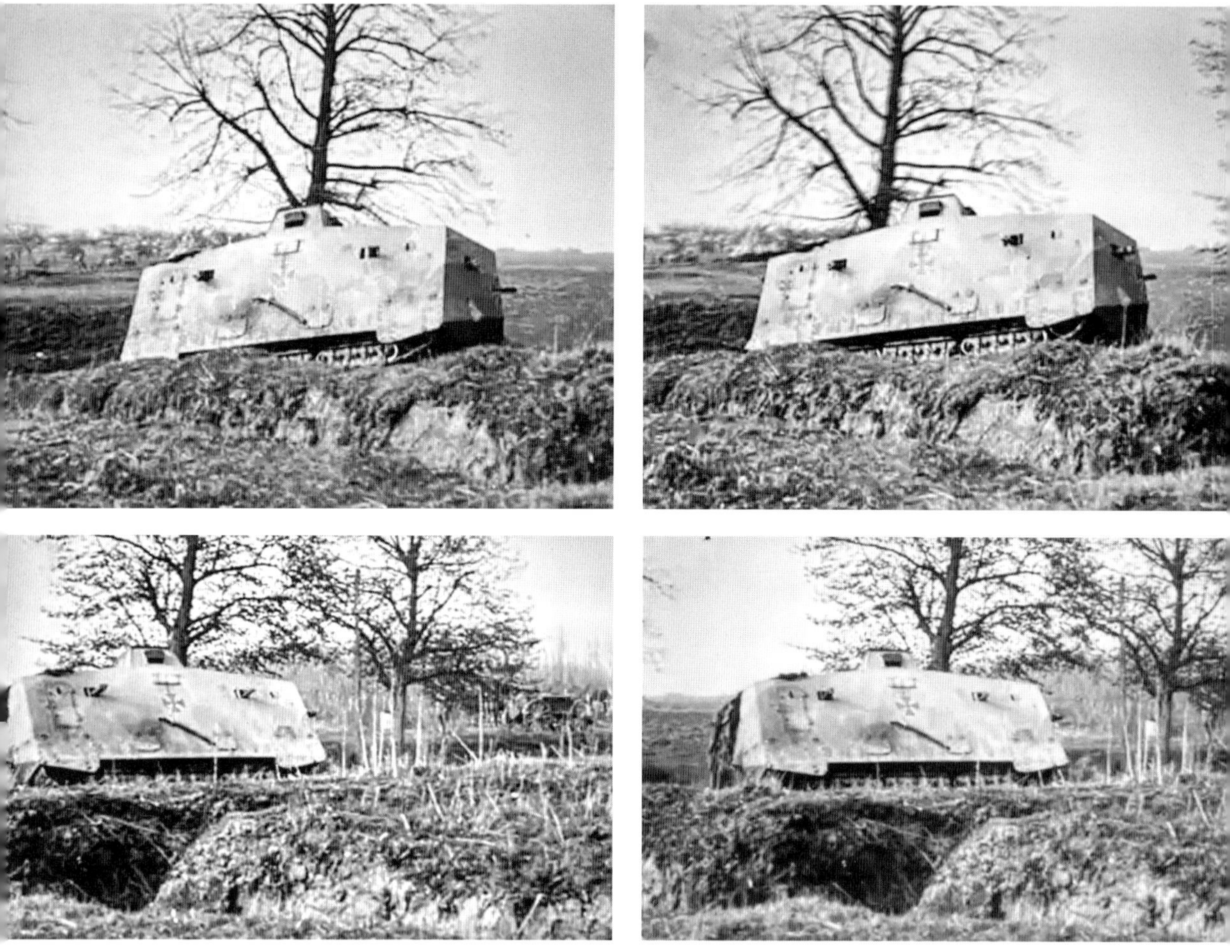

An A7V from Abteilung 1 pictured during the German spring offensive. (Bundesarchiv, Bild 183-P1013-316)

A7V 504, *Schnuck*, leading 528, *Hagen*. The latter was a standard 'second lot' vehicle originally manufactured in female configuration before receiving a 5.7-cm gun. Note the MG 08 machine guns in the side and rear of the tank.

A7V 528, *Hagen*, and crew. The vehicle later suffered the ignominy of sliding down a gully to evade friendly fire. Abandoned, it was captured by the New Zealand Division and later exhibited in London. (NARA)

Fourteen of the twenty A7Vs produced. The vehicle third from the left, chassis 541 was issued to Abteilung 1 in April 1918 and fought as the No. 3 tank at Villers-Bretonneux and subsequent attacks at Forêt de la Montagne de Reims on 18 July and Iwny on 11 October. Like many of its counterparts, the tank is thought to have been scrapped at the Erbenheim racecourse after the war.

A7V pair: 503, as *Faust*; 564, *Prinz Oskar*.

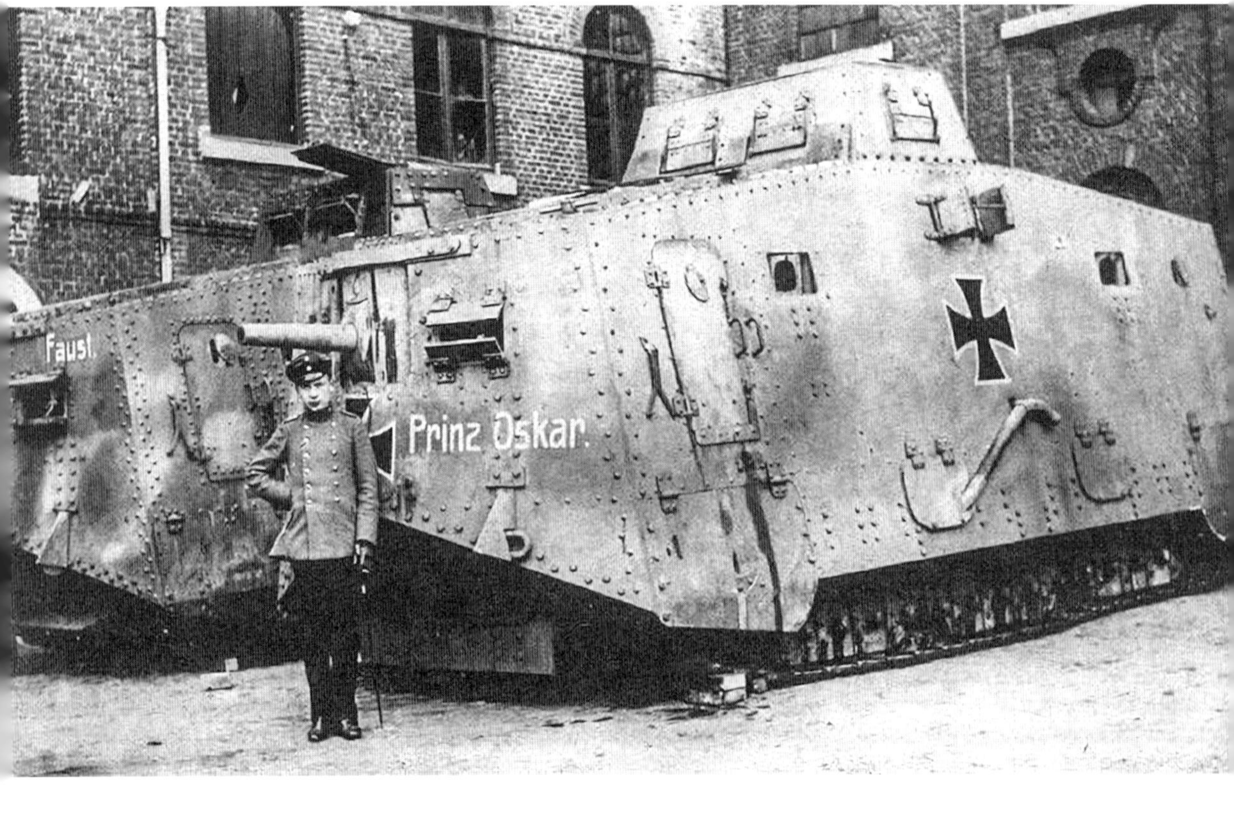

When not in combat, crewmembers would sit on the top of their vehicle to escape the heat and noise. This is A7V 504 *Schnuck*.

(**Below**) Newsreel footage of an Abteilung 2 pair under camouflage netting, the second vehicle possibly the No. 2 tank, 527.

Villers-Bretonneux – Tank Versus Tank

Unable to break through to the city of Amiens, a major rail junction, German forces targeted nearby Villers-Bretonneux and the strategically significant Hill 104. In the largest German armoured attack of the war, fifteen tanks were unloaded from a train at Guillaucourt on 21 April 1918. A7V 540, *Heiland*, had broken down prior to loading onto the train while 503's engine seized with a cracked cylinder head.

The remaining tanks and infantry advanced on the morning of 24 April behind a barrage of smoke, mustard gas and high explosive shells. There were three primary German thrusts – one into Villers-Bretonneux and surrounds with three tanks; a second with four tanks at the Bois d'Aquenne and two at the railway station; and a third towards Cachy with four tanks. 'Morale was high', Leutnant Ernst Volckheim, tank commander in both World Wars recalled, 'because for the first time we were driving into the enemy.' A British war correspondent was eyewitness to the German tanks: 'They looked like huge turtles, and their six machine guns … spat out bullets with vicious energy. They carried a small field-gun as well.' A British soldier narrowly escaped the onslaught:

> Having dealt with the front-line trench, the second tank turned and made for the writer's trench, and a third tank appeared, followed by German riflemen. The riflemen preceded to bayonet those men left in the front trench, and the third tank began to turn down the writer's trench from end to end.

British troops tried in vain to counter the German armour; drawing his revolver an officer fired futilely. Casualties mounted. One report stated: 'two tanks appeared (square Boche tanks) which cleared trench by firing pom-poms into our troops.'

'Heavy rifle and machine-gun on these tanks without effect', another officer of the 4th London Regiment (Royal Fusiliers) told.

> The tanks after some time managed to get astride our front-line trenches where they halted and opened enfilade fire down them. Having inflicted many casualties, they drove my men out of the front line, who withdrew about 500 yards, the enemy remaining in the position they had captured.

Nearby, Second Lieutenant Frank Mitchell's Mark IV male (No. 1 tank, No. 1 Section 'A Company', 1st Battalion Tank Corp) and two females moved off towards the village. An infantryman from the (inexperienced) British 8th Division suddenly appeared before Mitchell's vehicle, frantically waving his rifle: 'Look out! Jerry tanks about!' As Mitchell later wrote,

> I informed the crew [suffering from the effects of an earlier gas attack] and a great thrill ran through us all. Opening the loophole, I looked out. There, some

> 300 yards away, a round squat-looking monster was advancing. Behind it came waves of infantry and further away to left and right crawled two more of these armed tortoises. So we had met our rivals at last! For the first time in history tank was encountering tank!

Just after 7.00am the British 3rd Tank Brigade dispatched news of German forces 'employing four very large tanks.' An often-confusing armoured melee followed, typical of future tank-versus-tank encounters.

Mitchell's 6-pounder gunners fired two (failed) shots at the oncoming ememy tanks. In reply, a 'hurricane of hail' struck his machine, the 'interior filled with myriads of sparks and flying splinters ... the Jerry tank [A7V 561, *Nixe*] had treated us to a broadside of armour-piercing bullets!' Both females were hit by shells 'with great holes in their sides'. Mitchell pressed on. 'Another raking broadside of armour-piercing bullets gave us our first casualty, a bullet passing through the fleshy part of both legs of the Lewis gunner after piercing the side of the tank'. The unfortunate machine gunner lay on the tank's floor 'bleeding and groaning whilst the 6-pounder boomed over his head and the empty shell cases clattered all round him.'

With the sighting telescope vibrating on the unsprung vehicle, Mitchell 'took a risk and stopped the tank.' The pause was 'justified'.

> ... a well-aimed shot hit the enemy's conning tower, bringing him to a standstill. Another roar and yet another white puff at the front of the tank denoted a second hit! Peering with swollen eyes through his narrow slit, the gunner shouted words of triumph that were drowned by the roar of the engine. Then once more he aimed with great deliberation and hit for the third time. Through a loophole I saw the tank heel over to one side; then a door opened, and out ran the crew. We had knocked the monster out!

Mitchell's other gunners 'poured volley after volley into the retreating [German] figures.' He later watched as seven Mark A Whippet tanks arrived, scattering the enemy infantry. Losing a track to a hit from another German tank, Mitchell and crew 'crept gingerly out of the tank, the wounded man riding on the back of a comrade.'

Writing From the German perspective, Leutnant Wilhelm Biltz narrated how, 'on 24 April 1918, around 12 noon, I was in combat with the English garrisons on the outskirts of the village, 700 to 800 metres north-east of Cachy' when enemy troops appeared from nearby Aquenne Wood. Tanks [also] burst forth. The number of enemy tanks, the infantry later said, were eight. The first three tanks were the usual English type [Mark IV], the closest one opened fire.' Caught broadside, Biltz swung his tank in the direction of the English machines, allowing his gunners to take aim. 'When the first one [Mitchell's tank] just reached road leading out of Cachy to the north [and] stopped', Biltz believed it was negotiating a road ditch, his gunners scored a hit.

'Immediately afterwards, my tank received a direct hit (calibre about 6cm) to the right of the gun, killing one man and injuring two more.' With the rest of his crew having evacuated the tank, 'my vehicle received two more direct hits on the side.' Returning to his tank Blitz and his drivers were able to nurse the battered tank for 2.5km with leaking radiators and oil tanks before both engines failed.

Leutnant Bitter (525) recalled meeting British Whippet tanks for the first time: 'Appearance of tank – different from the well-known shape of the English tanks. It roughly corresponds to our tracked vehicles, with a four-sided armoured box in the centre; speed 15–20km per hour.' In the 20–25-minute battle, Bitter was 1km from Cachy when seven tanks appeared. Opening fire on one 'approaching at high speed' some 200m away, the first shot struck the Whippet's track, a second struck the centre of vehicle, with flames shooting high from the superstructure. Another Whippet 700m distant was also hit, though Bitter's main gun was now inoperable due to firing pin failure. His machine gunners swept and immobilized a third Whippet. The four remaining tanks, Bitter recounted, 'fled as quickly as possible in direction of Cachy'. The Whippet commander, Captain Price, reported being targeted by a field artillery; he had failed to spot the German machines.

In a well-planned and executed night attack, the Australian 13th and 15th Brigades recaptured Villers-Bretonneux on the night of 24–25 April.

Ernst Volckheim claimed victory. In his opinion, the 'Germans had demonstrated their superiority over British tanks.' A subsequent Order of the Day from Captain Friedrich Bornschlegel proclaimed: 'The 24th of April was a day of honour for the new combat branch.'

> Thanks to thorough preparation, the great energy and extraordinary courage of all acting officers, NCOs and troopers, all missions were accomplished. The tanks played a great part in the success of the day … The new combat branch has been victorious in its first major engagement and has proved that in its ranks lives the German spirit of 1914 which led the Germans from victory to victory in those August days.

'The enemy was considerably assisted by tanks', British intelligence summarised:

> According to prisoner's statements, these [tanks] were, in some instances, allotted on a scale of three per regiment and were intended to deal with strong points and machine-gun nests. The tanks apparently followed the infantry and came into action if the latter could make no progress … the personnel does not appear to have been well trained, as they repeatedly failed to take advantage of good targets, the machine guns were but little used, and in two instances the crew was seen to abandon the tank.

Noting what it believed was the first use of 'German-made tanks', a French 1st Army Bulletin reported: 'The general appearance is that of a tortoise surmounted by a turret. The caterpillar treads are protected by a shell. They are large, being about 10 metres long … They are heavily armed and carry two or three guns of about 37mm calibre. Witnesses are not unanimous on their machine-gun equipment, some stating two or four guns.'

The cover of Ernst Volckheim's *Deutsche Kampfwagen greifen an* ('German Tanks Attack'), a reprint of *Die deutschen Kampfwagen im Weltkriege*, featured German war artist Hugo Ungewitter's patriotic drawing of A7V Sturmpanzers advancing in the Battle of Villers-Bretonneux and Cachy.

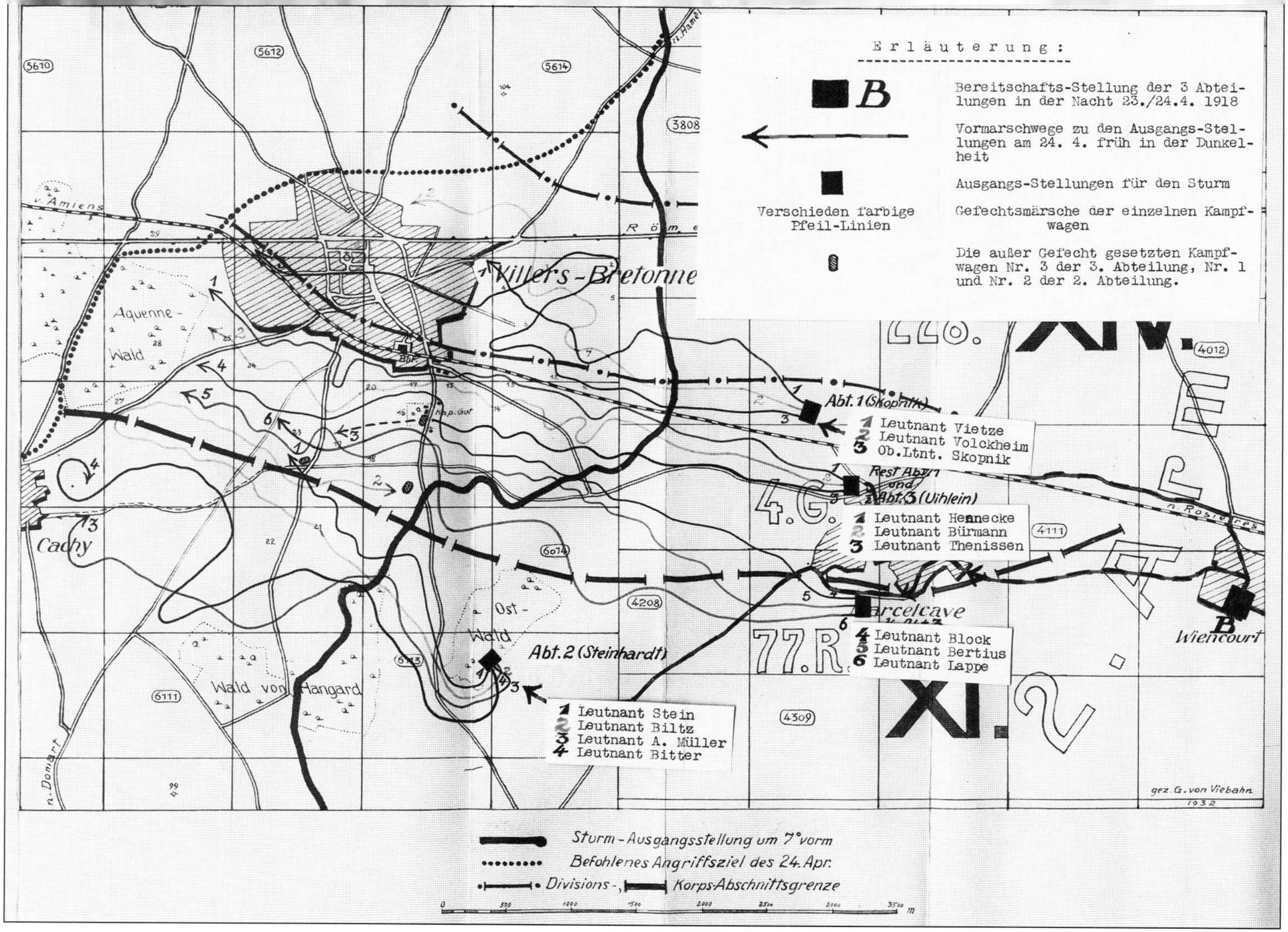

Starting position of the thirteen available German tanks during the night of 23–24 April 1918 and their advance routes the following morning before dawn. The Germans concluded from the battle that 'tanks have to work in close cooperation with infantry not only in attack but also in defense', noting that the British counterattack would not have been achieved had a tank reserve been available.

British Whippets at Villers-Bretonneux.

'A German Sturmwagen "cleans out" a French village' by painter and university professor Anton Hoffmann.

A7V 561, *Nixe*, was issued to Abteilung 2 in early April 1918 as its No. V vehicle. Raked by two the British Mark IV females, it was hit several times by Mitchell's Mark IV male No. 4066. Leutnant Wilhelm Biltz later nursed the vehicle 2.5km from the fighting. Three of his crew were dead, three others were injured. With salvage impossible, 561 was blown up on the night of 24/25 April. Abteilung 2 received 529 as a replacement, dubbed *Nixe II*. (AWM PO1726.002)

Another view of 561 post demolition, demonstrating the composite nature of the A7V – an armoured 'box' atop a tracked chassis. (Australian Army Museum of Western Australia)

Seen here in French hands, Leutnant Stein's A7V 542, *Elfriede*, was also lost outside Villers-Bretonneux. In the words of a German report: 'Tank No. 1 (Leutnant Stein) advanced with the first infantry wave, silencing number of machine guns and clearing up several sections of trench. At 9.45am, however, the tank ran onto a patch of undermined ground, turned over on its right side and was thus out of action. The crew, under the orders of the commander, left the tank and took part in the infantry battle as Sturmtruppen with three machine guns.' Only two crew members survived – one returned to German lines, the other was captured. Note the tank's final drives, visible below chassis level, a feature compromising ground clearance.

WHEN TANK MEETS TANK.

During the recent big advance on the Western front, British and German tanks met face to face. Two of the tanks engaged in a regular "hand-to-hand" fight. Eventually the British tank hurled itself upon its German adversary with such violence that the shell of the Hun tank was utterly smashed.

British media depictions of the historic first tank-versus-tank clash. In a later account of the battle understood to written by Lieutenant Frank Mitchell, the author affirmed: 'To sum up the battle, I consider that it was a great day for the German tanks, in fact their Cambrai. Their attack was a complete surprise and without their help the German infantry would not have taken Villers-Bretonneux or entered the Bois d'Aquenne. All the tanks, with the exception of the breakdowns, reached their objectives and returned to their rallying points.'

The War Illustrated, 15th June, 1918.

Regd. as a Newspaper & for Canadian Magazine Post.

The War Illustrated

No. 200

VOL. 8 [Weekly Nos. 193–208]

EDITED BY J. A. HAMMERTON

THREEPENCE

WHEN TANK MEETS TANK

An Incident in the Great Battle on the Western Front when German Tanks First Appeared in Action

LA DOMENICA DEL CORRIERE

Si pubblica a Milano ogni Domenica

Supplemento illustrato del "Corriere della Sera,,

MILANO

Per tutti gli articoli e illustrazioni è riservata la proprietà letteraria e artistica, secondo le leggi e i trattati internazionali.

Anno XX. — Num. 24. 16 - 23 Giugno 1918. Centesimi 10 il numero.

La guerra dei mostri. In Francia il primo scontro di tanks è avvenuto a Villers-Bretonneux.
Un " tank „ tedesco fu messo fuori combattimento da un " tank „ britannico di nuovo modello.

(Disegno di A. Beltrame).

Italy's weekly *La Domenica del Corriere* reported on the 'war of monsters' with a German tank knocked out [*sic*] by a 'new model' tank, the British Whippet.

A7V 506, *Mephisto*, carried an image of Mephistopheles, a demon featured in German folklore, holding a British tank under one arm. The image on the right is from the restored vehicle at Queensland Museum, Brisbane, Australia. Other mythological A7V names included *Siegfried*, *Wotan*, *Cyklop* and *Herkules*.

Leutnant Ernst Volckheim (fifth from the left) stands before A7V 560 following the Villers-Bretonneux battle on 24 April 1918. Originally issued to Abteilung 1 on 2 April 1918, the vehicle was later disabled by a shell prior to the fighting near Roye on 9 June. Successfully participating in the battle near Montagne de Reims on 15 July and an exercise with Bavarian Assault Battalion 6 on 22 August, the tank broke down during an approach march near Frémicourt. Later transported to an area near Cambrai, the tank joined an attack near Iwuy on 11 October. Breaking a track and unable to be salvaged, 560 was blown up to prevent capture.

Another view of Volckhiem's tank, 560, post Villers-Bretonneux. The Totenkopf insignia was unique to Abteilung 1 vehicles.

Abteilung 3's three remaining tanks – (left to right) 505, *Baden I*; 507, *Cyklop*; and 501, *Gretchen* – at Rosières-en-Santerre on 28 April 1918 following the earlier loss of 506, *Mephisto*, and 540, which had broken down a week earlier. (AWM C04603)

The crew of A7V 505, draped in camouflage netting, pose with their musical instruments. The signs at the bottom read: 'Tank 505 orchestra' and 'Today – First Class Artist Concert – Entry Free'. This vehicle was unable to participate at St Quentin after burnt-out clutches and frozen gears prevented it from reaching the enemy line. Transferred from Abteilung 1 to Abteilung 2, it was named *Baden I* and fought at Villers-Bretonneux. (AWM C04604)

A7V 529, *Nixe II*, was abandoned outside Reims on 31 May 1918 after French 75-mm artillery shells penetrated the left and rear armour, destroying the gearbox. German attempts to recover the vehicle failed.

A7V 505, *Baden I*, and crew. Renamed *Prinz August Wilhelm*, later shortened to *August Wilhelm*, the vehicle fought at Reims and Roye. Unable to be repaired at BAKP 20 in late 1918 because of the facility's relocation, the tank is believed to have been sent to Erbenheim, where it was found by the French and scrapped.

(**Opposite, above**) Several Beutepanzer Mark IV tanks and an A7V in transit by rail. Although the A7Vs performed well, Operation *Michael* ultimately failed to deliver its intended knockout blow. The official German history later ascribed the failure of the offensive, despite some remarkable early gains, in part, to a lack of anti-tank weapons, too few tanks, a lack of trucks and a paucity of railroads to the frontlines.

(**Opposite, below**) *Hagen* and *Schnuck* advance through a smoke screen in a village near Rheims in 1918. French authorities concluded after Villers-Bretonneux that the 'tactical use of tanks does not seem definitely regulated in the German army as yet. Perhaps the minor operations attempted till now are only experiments to prepare the entrance into line, under favourable circumstances, of tank formations now in training.' (NARA)

(**Above**) Machine guns removed, A7V 563, *Wotan*, is driven up a railway loading ramp. Note the partially collapsed central cupola, which could be folded to meet rail transport height requirements. A German report logged that the A7V Abteilungen were based at Charleroi and transferred to combat assignments via the army rail system. 'Since there was extensive activity in Charleroi, civilian Belgian workers were also employed in the parks and workshops. The Entente used them to conduct extensive espionage … the railway journey on 19 April [to near Villers-Bretonneux] was disrupted and delayed by numerous bombing raids.' (NARA)

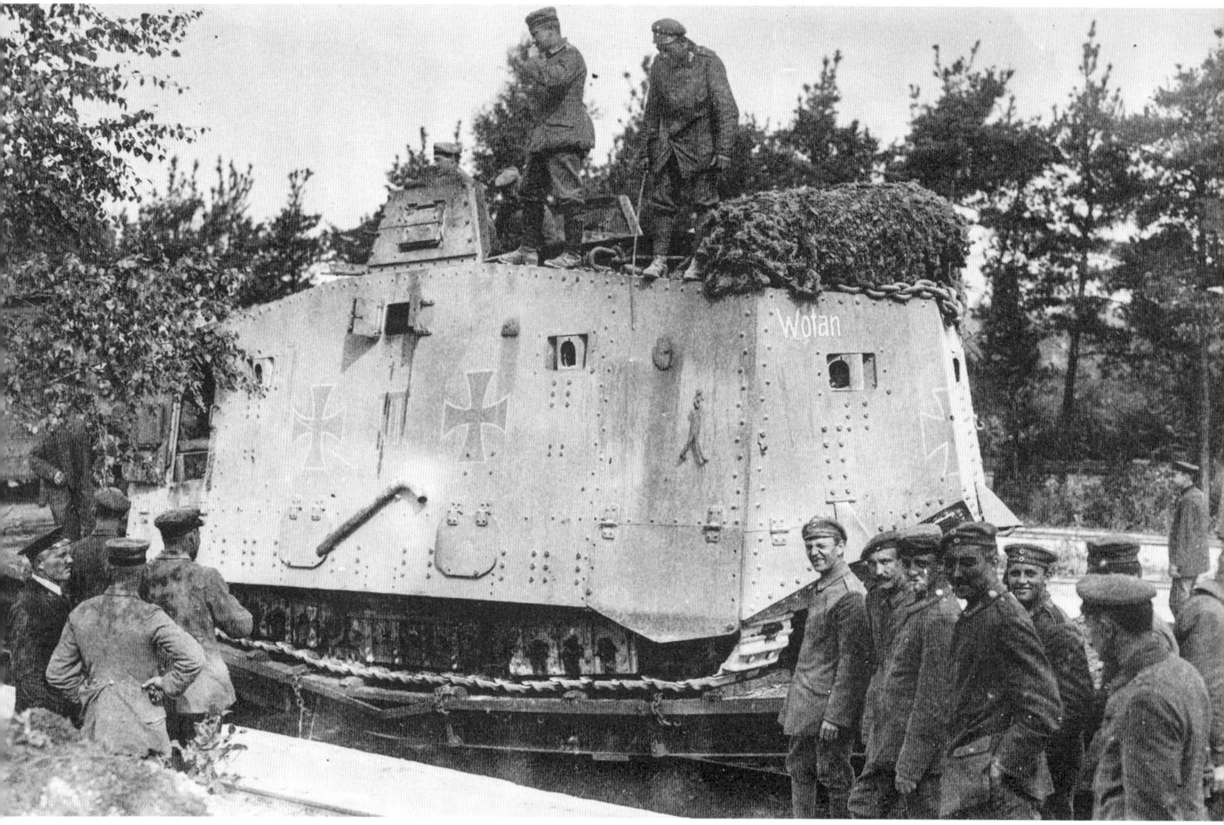

The dusty *Wotan* appears to have been too heavy for the ramp. Note the camouflage netting on the rear of the vehicle. Assigned to Abteilung 2 as its No. 3 vehicle and christened *Wotan* following the loss of 542 *Elfriede*, it participated in several battles including an attack near Iwuy, in northern France. (NARA)

Wotan was (presumably) scrapped at the Erbenheim racecourse at war's end.

Three A7Vs from Abteilung 2, which completed its training on 22 March 1918, at a railhead (left to right): 504, *Schnuck*, 563, *Wotan*, and 525, *Siegfried*, in June 1918. Note the circular escape hatch on the rear of the nearest vehicle. A7V 525 was assigned to Abteilung 2, as vehicle No. 2, in early April 1918 and dubbed *Siegfried* prior to the fighting at Villers-Bretonneux on 24 April 1918 where its crew claimed to have destroyed three Whippet tanks. It fought at Reims the following month and again in the forest at Montagne de Reims on 15 July. Breaking down before an attack near Frémicourt on 31 August, the tank was repaired and participated in several marches north of Cambrai and in the Iwuy fighting on 11 October 1918. It is believed the vehicle also ended up at Erbenheim to escape capture and was later scrapped.

One of the Abteilung 2 tanks with crew riding on top. Starting the A7V's two large engines due to inferior grade fuel proved problematic, especially during the winter months. Consequently, various starting devices were used: (a) priming pump, (b) electric starter, (c) Bosch atomizer, (d) three-man hand crank, (e) acetylene. Once one engine was started, it could be used to start the second one through the transmission.

Cyklop

(**Opposite, above**) A7V 507 had an inauspicious beginning in Abteilung 1, breaking down before reaching British lines on 21 March 1918 and later sliding off a rail wagon on 27 March. Following repairs at BAKP 20, the vehicle was reassigned to Abteilung 3 and named *Cyklop*. After Villers-Bretonneux it was renamed *Prinz Eitel Friedrich* (later shortened to *Eitel Friedrich*) in June 1918. Following an engagement near Roye on 9 June, the vehicle was shipped to Saarburg for familiarisation training where it remained until 4 October. Presumed to have been later relocated to *Kampfwagen Abteilung Körting* barracks near Berlin, it saw Freikorps service in the 1919 uprising, tagged *Imperator*.

(**Opposite, below**) A7V 507 caught in a ditch on a training ground outside Saarburg, on 31 August 1918.

(**Above**) Abteilung 2 A7Vs and crew, (right to Left) 504, *Schnuck*; 525, *Siegfried*; and possibly, 563 and 528. (NARA)

(**Below**) A7V 543, seen here as *Aldabert*, initially served with Abteilung 2 as its No. 4 vehicle. It was later transferred to Abteilung 3 in May 1918 as a replacement for 501, *Gretchen*. Immediately above the seated soldier is one of the upward opening tow hooks covers.

German soldiers camouflage A7V 501, *Gretchen* against Allied air observation. Pictured here at the Sachy training ground near Sedan, France, in October 1918 during the filming of the propaganda film *Die Abwehrschlacht* ('The Defensive Battle'). (AWM H13460 & H13459)

Rear and front views of A7V 501 (now armed with a 5.7cm gun) displaying the Balkenkreuz symbol, in place of the earlier Tatzenkreuz emblem, plus Totenkopf death's head symbol. This tank was later abandoned at a railhead at the Belgium village of Sainte-Cécile. (AWM H13458 & H13461)

A7V 501 just weeks away from war's end.

An A7V pair provide the backdrop for a portrait of German troops and French prisoners.

The German spring offensive had stalled by the summer of 1918. German tanks were reported in small numbers on other occasions, though the tide of war had long since turned. The initiative now lay with the Allies whose soldiers fought well-coordinated battles supported by the latest tanks, artillery and aircraft, a precursor to the highly mobile campaigns of the Second World War. In the weeks before the Armistice on 11 November 1918, all three A7V formations, as well as the Mark IV Beutepanzer formations (see Chapter 7) were transferred from Charleroi to Erbenheim, in Germany, and disbanded on 17 November.

Future General der Panzertruppe ('General of the Armoured Corps') Hermann Balck, who had served as infantry officer in the First World War, ruminated on the defeat, writing: 'Ludendorff's decision to attack in 1918 has since been criticized, because in the end it did not punch through, although there were some initial successes. Ludendorff wanted to defeat the English and the French before the Americans could be in position at full strength.'

Reflecting on his wartime efforts to establish an armoured force, Ludendorff conceded: 'Perhaps I ought to have made greater efforts; and possibly we should in

Formerly *Lotti* during the fighting at Villers-Bretonneux. 527 later became the No. 2 tank of Abteilung 1 denoted by the number-in-the-circle insignia on the hull side.

Veteran of battles at Villers-Bretonneux and near Roye and St Etienne, 503, is believed to have been scrapped at the Erbenheim racecourse after the Armistice. Note the Balkenkreuz outlined in white to aid identification.

that case have had a few more tanks for the decision in 1918; but I do not know what other claim could have been set aside to enable them to be built. We could not release any more workmen, and the people at home could not supply any more. Had any been available, we should have wanted them as recruits. We should never have been able to put masses of tanks into action in 1918 – and tanks are effective only in masses.'

Leading A7V Tank Actions

Date	*Battle*	*No. of Abt.*	*No. of tanks*
21 March 1918	St Quentin	1	5
24 April 1918	Villers-Bretonneux	3	13
1 June 1918	Soissons	1	5
1 June 1918	Reims	1	5
9 June 1918	River Matz	2	10
31 August 1918	Frémicourt	1	5
11 October 1918	North of Cambrai	1	5

Chapter Six

'An armoured caterpillar carrying a 6-pounder gun and six machine guns'

Several A7V tanks fell into Allied hands during the fighting of 1918. Duly examined and exhibited, only one of these machines, 506, *Mephisto*, survives today with the remainder scrapped.

Elfriede

Elfriede, 542, was the first German tank to be captured by Entente forces. A German raiding party had failed to destroy the tank and it was chanced upon by scouting

Elfriede and crew. (NARA)

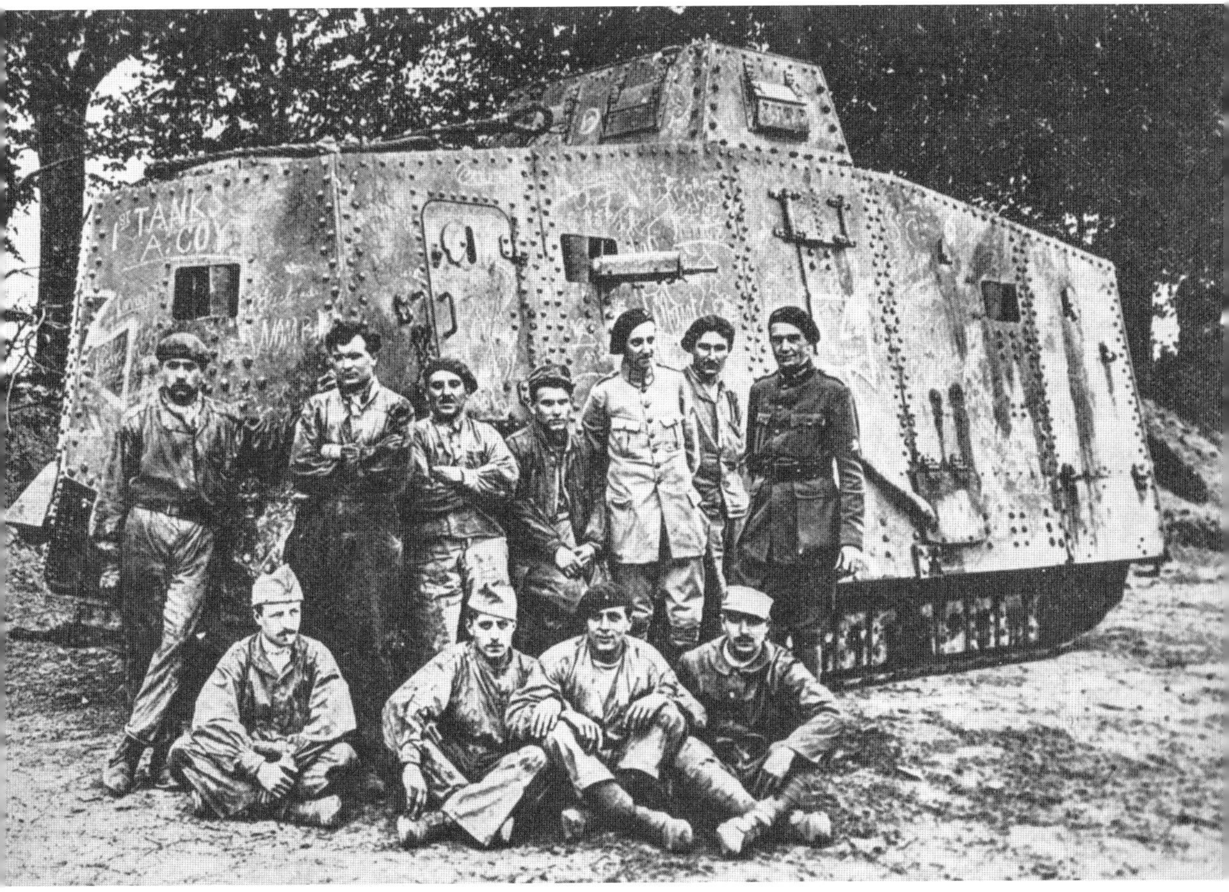

parties from the French 37th Moroccan Division. Lying on its side in a quarry on 2 May, it had overturned during the fighting around Villers-Bretonneux on 24 April 1918. Moroccan troops were unable to recover the vehicle. Inspected by the intelligence department of the *Grand Quartier Général* it was salvaged by the French *Section de Ravitaillement et de Réparation* with assistance of two British Mark V tanks. After examining the tank, a French Army Bulletin, dated 6 May 1918, detailed:

> The tank has three compartments: (1) A forward compartment, about 3m long, contains two machine guns (one on each side) and has in front a 57mm gun supplied with HE shells and shrapnel (at least 100 projectiles). (2) A rear compartment 2.5m long, contains four machine guns; one on each side and two in rear. (3) A central compartment, about 1.2m long contains the driving and steering mechanism: two 100hp 6-cylinder Daimler-Mercedes motors furnish the power; above are the two drivers' seats behind which are two gasoline tanks holding 180–200 litres each. This compartment has a turret which permits the pilot to see to steer.

'The German tank', the communiqué concluded, 'is mechanically very carefully constructed and is unquestionably very rapid and powerful owing to its two motors which develop over 200hp.' Yet,

> It does not seem to have great facility in passing over obstacles; the form of the caterpillar track would not permit crossing an obstacle wider than 2m. The armour which comes down very close to the ground greatly hinders operations on heavy and muddy ground. Finally, the armament (a single gun of small calibre) is far from being in relation to the mass or power. It is [a] little vulnerable in front and the tank must be combatted by attempts to reach its sides (particularly the central portion and the position of the gasoline tanks), the rear, the turret, the sighting plates and above all when it uncovers all of its lower part while crossing an obstacle.

Elfriede shortly after capture. The original roman numerals would shortly be replaced by a '3' representing the French 3° Tirailleurs.

SKETCH OF A GERMAN TANK CAPTURED ON APRIL 24th,

SOUTH OF VILLERS-BRETTONNEUX.

Scale approx. 1/50.

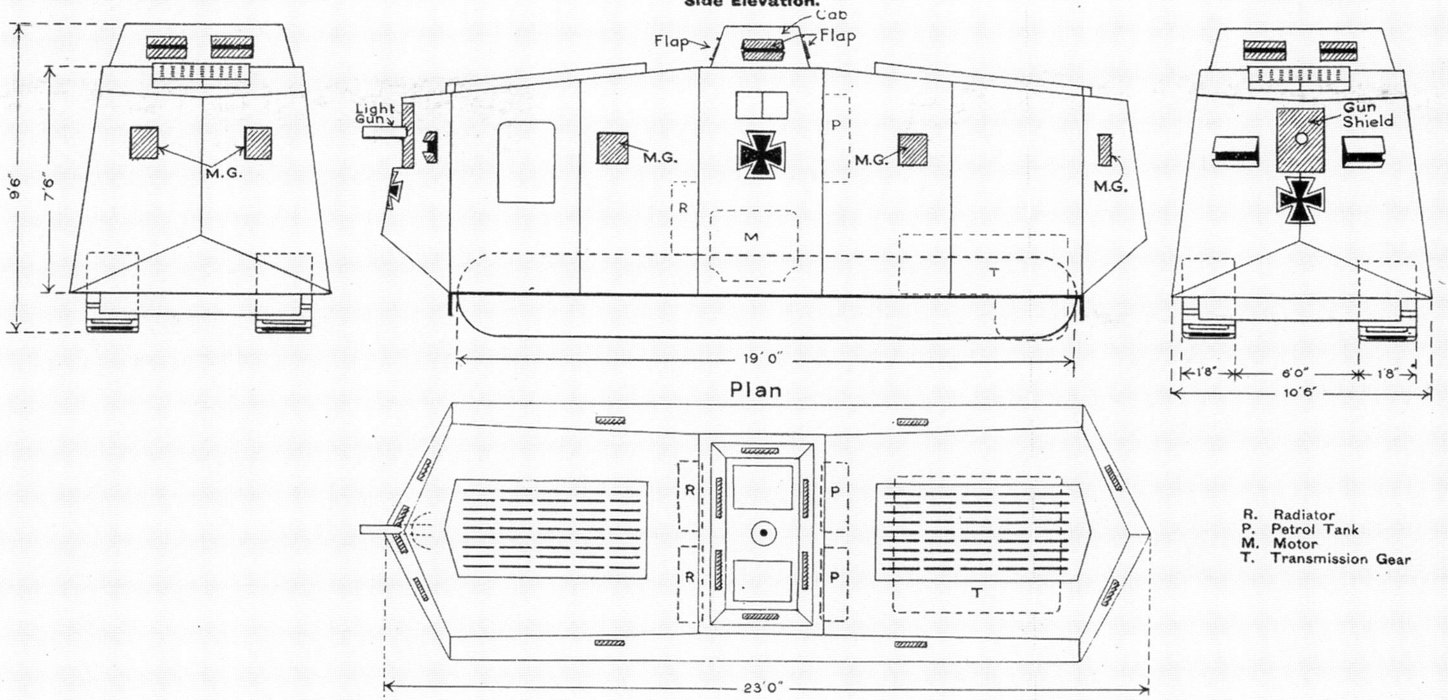

NOTES.

Points most vulnerable to Rifle and Machine Gun bullets shown hatched in red.

French A.P. bullets have penetrated the cab. Ordinary bullets pass through apertures if flap is open, and through space between Gun Shield and front of Tank.

The "splash" of ordinary bullets is effective against cab, and against Machine Gun emplacements. Armour Plate is of poor quality, and there is no protection against the "splash" of an ordinary bullet.

This Tank cannot cross a large trench (8 feet or over) or large shell holes.

FIELD SURVEY CO., R.E. (3582) 10-5-18.

ARTILLERY.

A direct hit will put this Tank out of action. The most favourable moment for firing at the Tank is when in crossing an obstacle, it exposes its under-carriage. This is undoubtedly its most vulnerable part.

Above Drawings are made from direct measurements of an actual Tank and from Photographs of same.

VIOLENTE ATTAQUE LOCALE DES ALLEMANDS. — LE TRAITÉ DE BUCAREST

EXCELSIOR

Jeudi 9 MAI 1918

RÉDACTION & ADMINISTRATION
20, rue d'Enghien, 20 — PARIS (X^e)
Téléphone : Gutenberg 02.73 - 02.75 - 15.00
Adresse télégraphique : EXCEL-PARIS

TARIF DES ABONNEMENTS :
France...... 3 mois, 10 fr. ; 6 mois, 18 fr. ; 1 an, 35 fr.
Étranger... 3 mois, 20 fr. ; 6 mois, 36 fr. ; 1 an, 70 fr.

PUBLICITÉ : 11, Bd des Italiens.-Tél. : Gut. 80-88

:: PIERRE LAFITTE, FONDATEUR ::

9e Année. — N° 2.732. — 10 centimes. — Étranger : 20 centimes.

« Le plus court croquis m'en dit plus long qu'un long rapport. » — NAPOLÉON

DEUX TANKS ALLEMANDS CAPTURÉS

Premières photos des chars d'assaut ennemis arrivées hier à Paris

TANK ALLEMAND CULBUTÉ DANS UNE CARRIÈRE, PRÈS DE VILLERS-BRETONNEUX. — ON VOIT ICI LE DESSUS ET LA TOURELLE

SOLDATS DU TIRAILLEURS MONTANT LA GARDE DEVANT UNE DES « CHENILLES » CAPTURÉES PAR LEUR RÉGIMENT

Lors des combats qui furent livrés au cours des dernières journées d'avril autour de Villers-Bretonneux, il fut donné aux combattants d'assister, pour la première fois, à un duel de tanks. L'affaire fut chaude. Mais elle ne tarda pas à tourner au désavantage de l'ennemi. Ecrasées par le feu de notre artillerie lourde, heurtées de front par les chars d'assaut franco-britanniques, les monstrueuses "chenilles" allemandes furent désemparées. Ces deux-ci s'échouèrent dans une carrière où elles furent capturées par nos fantassins.

Elfriede featured in the French newspaper *Excelsior* on 9 May 1918. Note the ventilation louvres which Allied examiners noted: 'consist of three layers of steel slats, spaced so as to admit a current of air', and coiled towing cable.

French weekly *Le Miroir* also showcased the prized A7V. Recounting the fighting at Villers-Bretonneux, Australian war correspondent C.E.W. Bean wrote: 'what happened to all the tanks … One of them certainly blundered into a quarry where some officers were stationed. It lay there afterwards half overturned, and Australians who saw it when an advanced party leader reached this point, say it was something like our own older classes of tanks, but if anything longer, the nose of it not a snub snout like that of our tanks, but having a sharp edge. The body extended the whole length of the tank, and there were loopholes along the sides just beneath the roof. The long caterpillar travellers on which it moved extended the whole length of the body but did not travel over the roof of the tank as well as under its belly.'

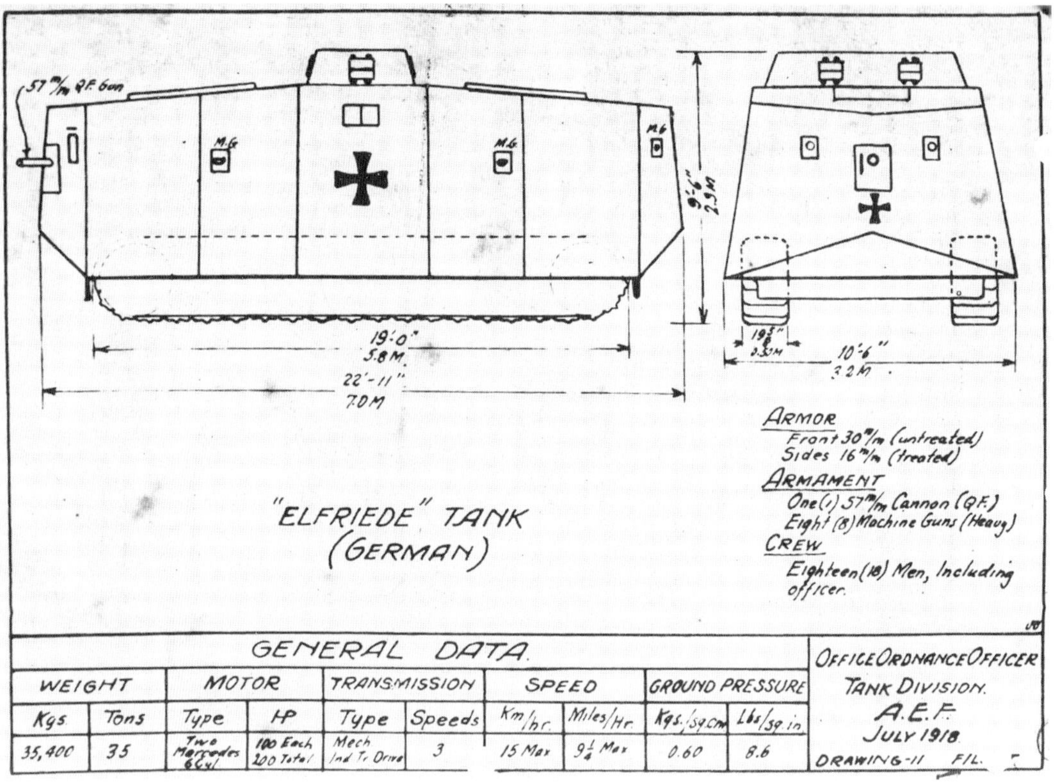

Allied intelligence drawing.

Elfriede, unlike *Mephisto*, had not been sabotaged and once righted was driven to Saleux, southwest of Amiens.

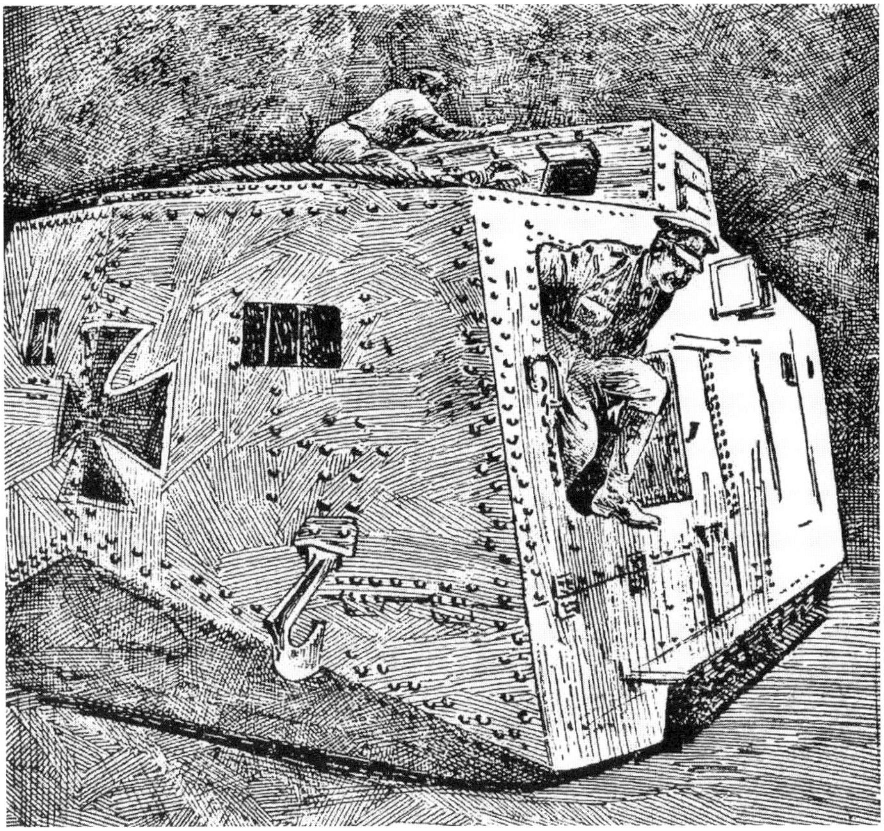

British newspapers condemned the machine. 'The much-heralded Panzerkraftwagen, or German tank', one announced in September 1918: '... made its debut in fair numbers in in the last great German attack. One of these tanks entered a stone quarry and turned over on its side, and a subsequent advance by French troops placed this German machine well within Allied lines where it could be studied at leisure. The German version of the tank is a ponderous affair, quite in keeping with the tendencies of the Teutons. It weighs 45 tons and carries a crew of eighteen. In general appearance it follows the French rather than the English design of tank but is far larger than anything yet attempted by the Allies with the exception of the American steam-driven tanks, which, up to date, have not yet been in action. Following the practice of the French and British tank crews, the Germans have named each of the Panzerkraftwagen. In the case of the captured tank, it bears the name "Elfriede", and carries on all sides the characteristic Maltese cross of the German air service. Its armour varies from 1.2 inches for the front plates to .64 inches on the sides and .8 inches at the rear. The metal employed must be applied in considerable thickness because of the evident lack of steel in Germany, and that in turn makes for a cumbersome, if not inefficient, tank. As for armament, one 47mm or 1.85-inch rapid fire cannon is mounted for direct fire ahead, and six machine guns mounted in pairs are placed at the sides and tie rear. The eighteen men of the crew have none too much room in this 23-foot tank, and the conditions during actual combat are certainly not unlike the proverbial sardines in a box. The conning tower, in which the driver sits is entered from above and has hinged side-shutters, but it is reported that observation even at moderate range is difficult owing to structural defects. The crew can get in or out of the steel box by means of two doors on either side. Every inch of space within the tank is utilised to the utmost; in fact folding chairs are mounted on the inside of the doors, and ropes are hanging from the ceiling in order to provide 'straps' for the crew after the fashion of a crowded tramcar. All in all, the Panzerkraftwagen, aside from an enclosed gear box which reduces the possibility of the gear getting clogged with mud and dirt, presents no improvement over French end British tanks which have fallen into the hands of the Germans. If anything, it is merely more cumbersome through lack of proper materials, and therefore a poorer fighter.'

(**Above**) An Australian soldier beside *Elfriede*, holed by four armour-piercing bullets to the left side of the iron cross insignia. The British Military Intelligence Section 2 (MI2), learned from a surviving *Elfriede* crewmember that the German tanks at Villers-Bretonneux were taken by rail to Wiencourt-l'Équipée (near Guillaucourt), on the night of 20–21 April, where they remained under camouflage until 4.00am on 24 April, when they moved forward by road. The prisoner's tank, it was noted, 'went into action in front of the infantry. It met with considerable rifle and machine gun fire, which kept down the fire of its own machine guns, as bullets passed through the apertures and wounded several of the gunners', including the prisoner, who was left behind.' (AWM E02369)

(**Opposite, above**) *Elfriede* seen covered in graffiti from passing British, Australian and French troops. Regarding its colour scheme, a captured German crewmember stated that 'tanks have an iron cross on the side. They are generally made more inconspicuous by splashes of multicolour paint and a screen of camouflage.' (AWM E02459)

(**Opposite, below**) Frontal view of *Elfriede* and its 57mm gun. Officially, the tank carried 180 shells, but crews sometimes carried more than 300 rounds – a mix of grapeshot, high-explosive and armour piercing.

Elfriede
III

Following is a series of five images taken by Sergeant Harry A. Hales, 10th Company, 2nd Regiment, Air Service Mechanics, who served with a US tank repair unit at Recloses, France.
(National WWI Museum and Memorial)

Elfriede.

Elfriede

Elfriede

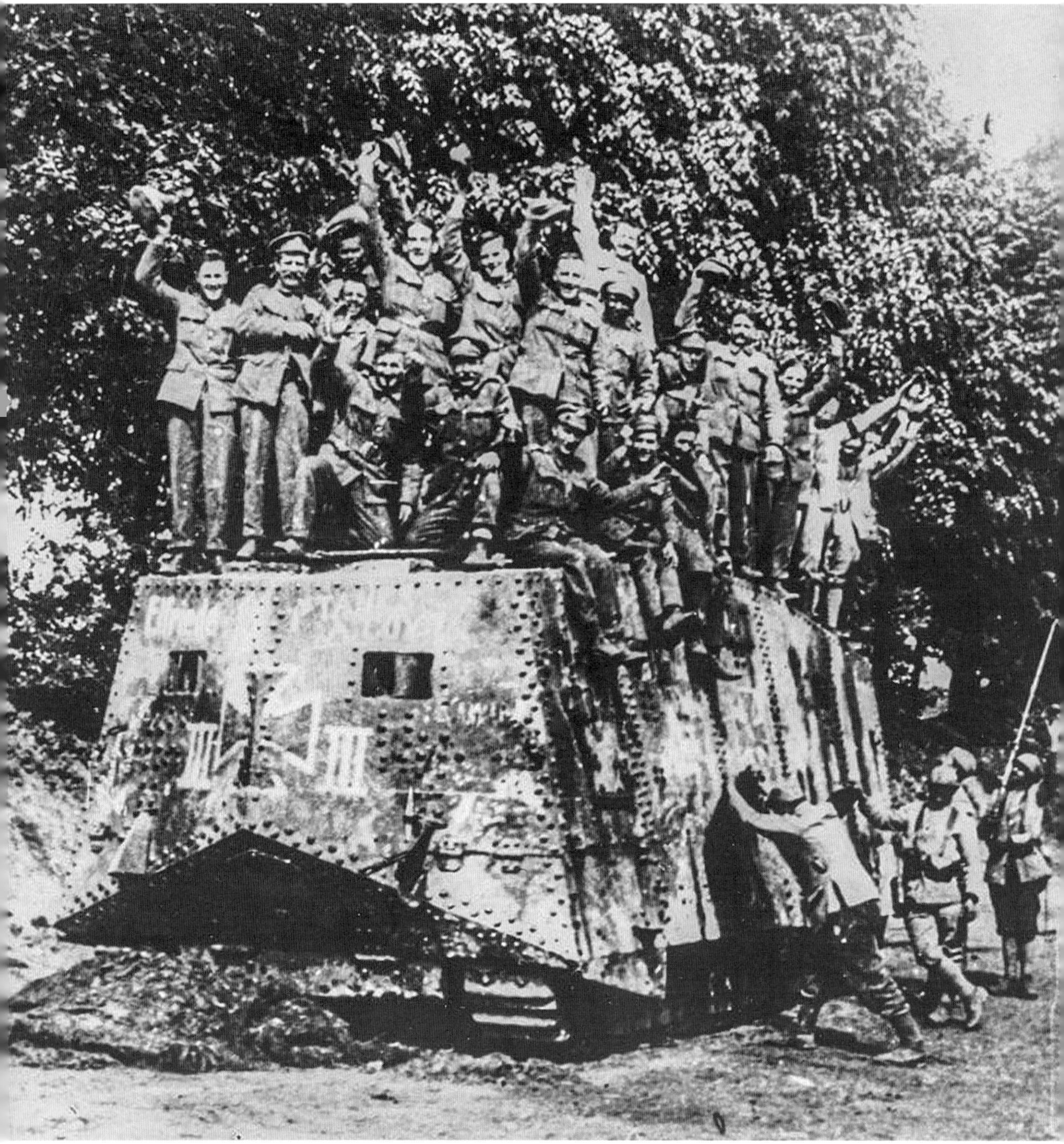

Allied soldiers celebrate *Elfriede*'s capture. An early Allied intelligence report stated: 'The German tank *Elfriede*, the first to be captured can be described as an armoured caterpillar carrying a 6-pounder gun and six machine guns. It can cross ordinary country (cornfields, roots, etc.) as fast as a trotting horse, but can neither cross an 8-foot trench nor climb a 4-foot bank.'

(**Above & over**) *Elfriede* was presented to Louis Breton (Under-Secretary of State for Inventions) on 18 May 1918, the event photographed and filmed by the *Section photographique des Armées.*

Elfriede

Elfriede

Elfriede

Transported by rail to Paris in early October 1918, the tank became a popular attraction.
(National WWI Museum and Memorial)

Elfriede was exhibited along with other spoils of war at the Place de la Concorde. (National WWI Museum and Memorial)

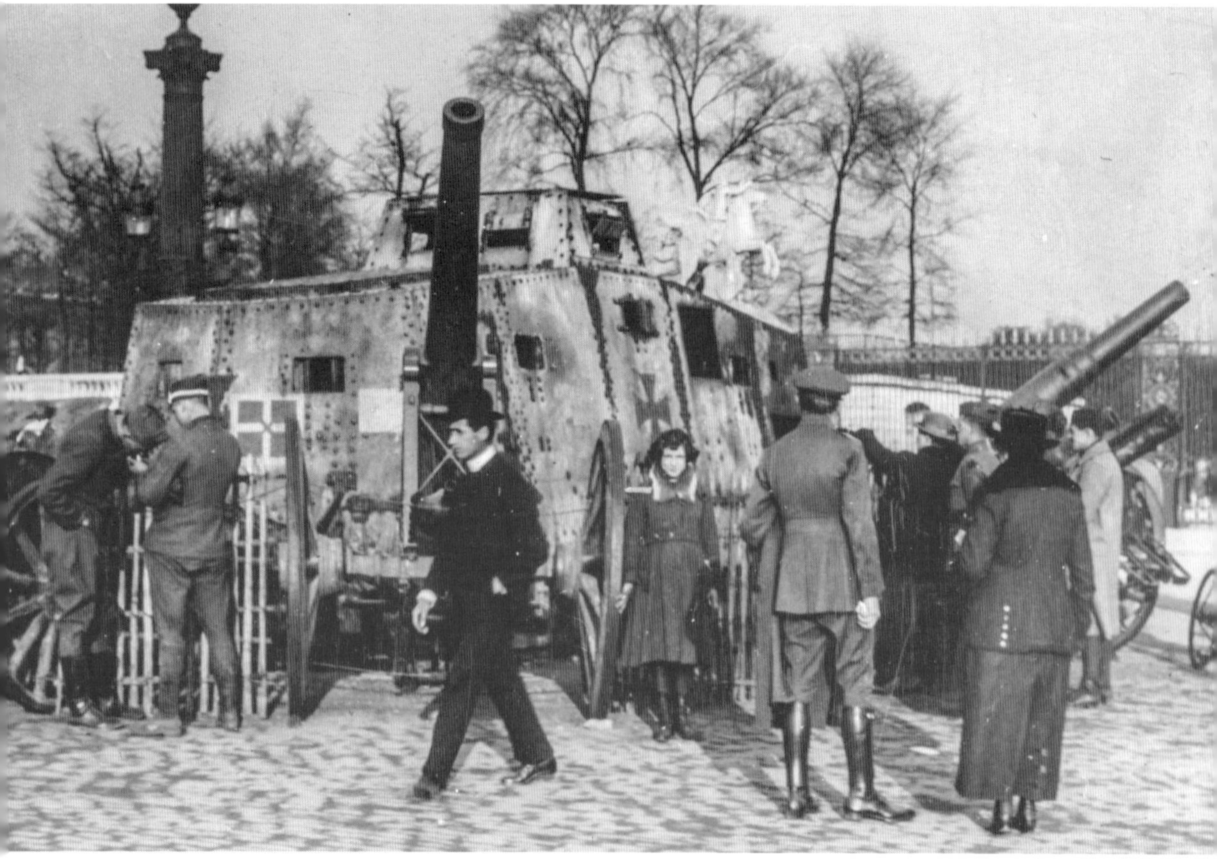

(**Below**) *Elfriede* behind a 21cm Lange Mörser M 16/L14.5, a heavy howitzer used by the German Army in both World Wars. Possibly transferred to a French training ground for further testing in early 1919, the tank was later scrapped. (National WWI Museum and Memorial)

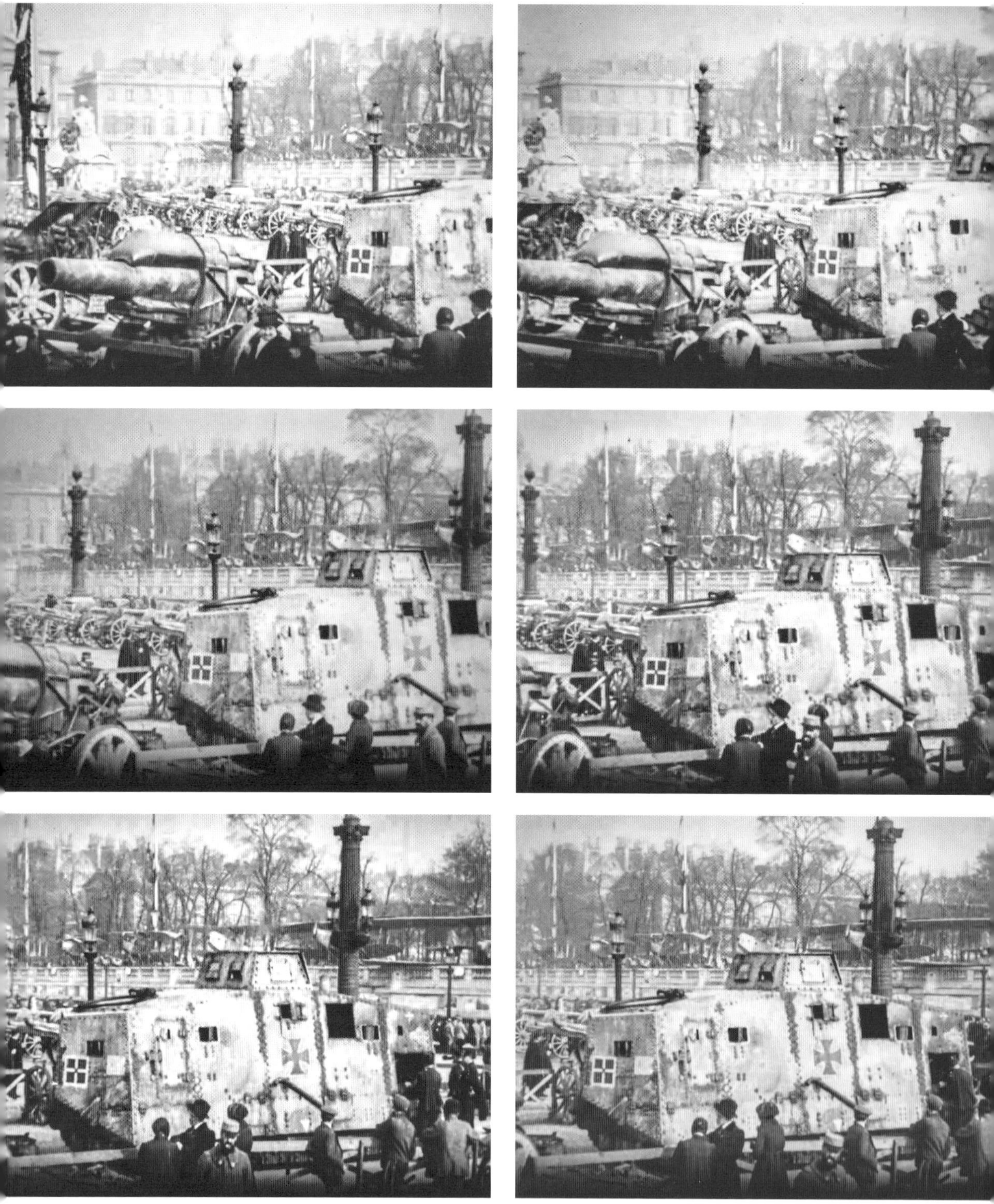

Newsreel footage of *Elfriede* and captured artillery. (NARA)

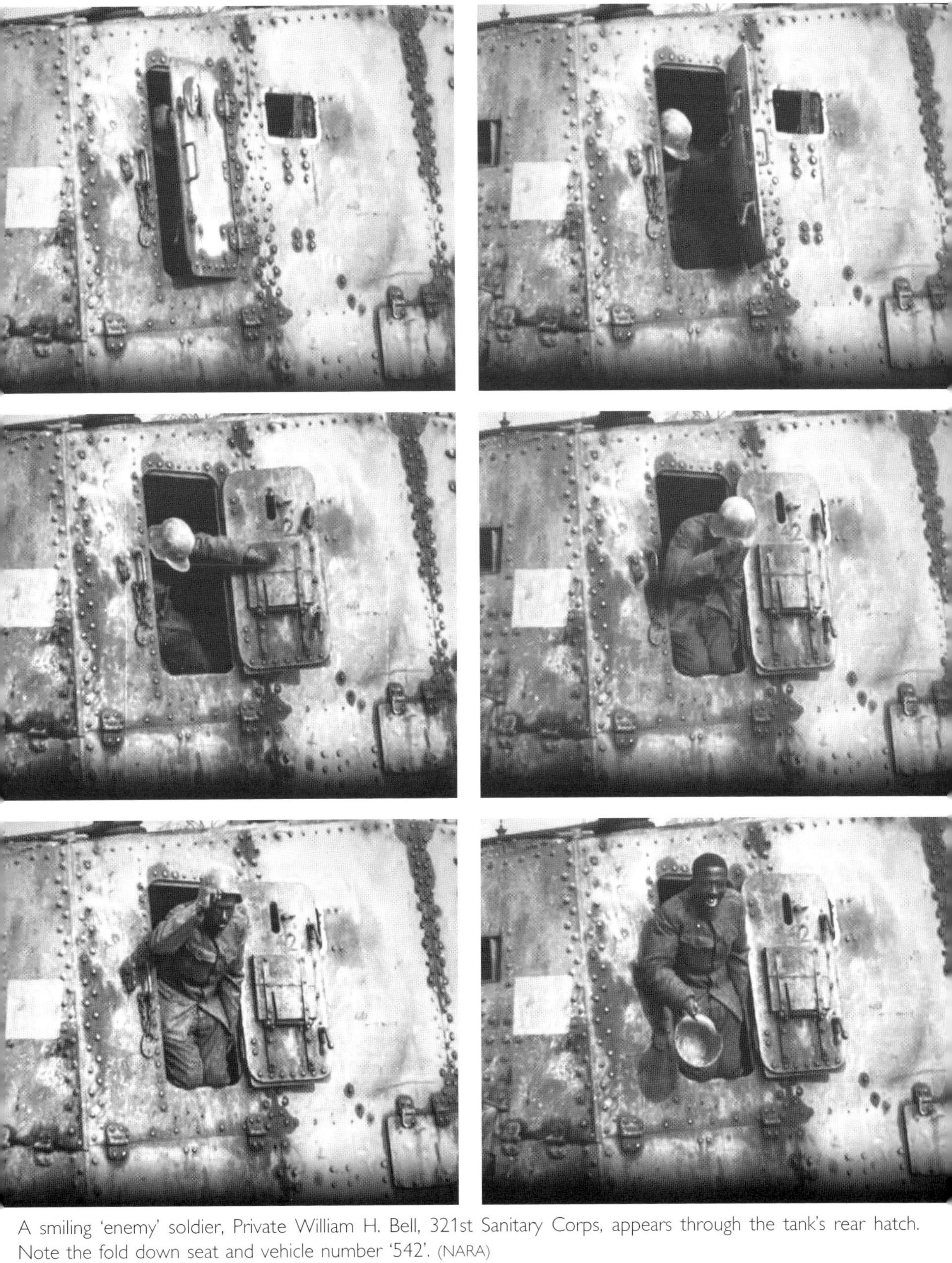

A smiling 'enemy' soldier, Private William H. Bell, 321st Sanitary Corps, appears through the tank's rear hatch. Note the fold down seat and vehicle number '542'. (NARA)

Joyous Parisian onlookers atop *Elfriede* during celebrations marking the return of Alsace-Lorraine to French rule, 17 November 1918.

Mephisto

A7V 506, *Mephisto*, suffered a series of mishaps during the fighting around Villers-Bretonneux. After a blocked fuel line and carburettor jets were cleared, the tank became stranded in shell crater. Salvage attempts proved unsuccessful and it remained *in situ* behind German lines. Describing it as 'a bulky cumbersome contrivance, larger than our tanks', Lieutenant-Colonel J.A. Robinson, officer commanding the 26th Battalion, AIF, narrated the elaborate plan to retrieve the enemy vehicle.

> Just before nightfall on the night of 14 July, a detachment of the 26th, aided by two successful bombing attacks, secured lengths of German trenches, at the same time pushing out several parties to protect the flanks. When darkness came the Australians dug in on a 1,500 yards front, 600 yards ahead of their previously vacated trenches. By that means they secured the whole of Monument Wood, a number of prisoners, arms and equipment, and *Mephisto*, the tank. In addition to the prisoners taken, a number of Germans were killed. Our casualties were one man wounded ... *Mephisto* was only 20 yards behind our trenches, and it had been arranged that two of the British tanks should tow it back. We realised, however, that the noise of the moving tanks would

immediately be heard by the Germans, who would attend to the position from which it came in the usual way. To overcome this difficulty, we arranged that during the period that the tanks were working aeroplanes should circle overhead, and the artillery keep up an intermittent fire to drown the noise. In a measure the plan was successful, for *Mephisto* was brought back. We were unfortunate, however, in selecting the night of 20 July to move it. On that night the Germans launched a huge gas attack in which 600 soldiers of the 6th (Victorian) Brigade, who were then holding the line, the tank crews, and the fatigue parties from the 26th were gassed. Still, we got *Mephisto* out, and by stages back to Vaux Wood, near Amiens. Here, since it was the first German 'land crab' that the British had captured, it became a great centre of interest, and was inspected by the high commands of the of Allied armies.

Anzac Bulletin

Issued to Members of the Australian Military and Naval Forces in Great Britain, France, and elsewhere; by Authority of the High Commissioner for Australia.

Edited by Capt. H. C. SMART.

No. 89 (New Issue). LONDON, SEPTEMBER 20, 1918. Price 3d.

German tank captured by an Australian Battalion.

(*Australian Official Photograph*).

Despite British authorities wishing to retain possession of the tank, which featured on the front page of the *Anzac Bulletin*, policy allowing AIF units to retain possession of war trophies saw the vehicle transported to Australia.

Guarding *Mephisto*. 'We know how to stop the super-tank', a British newspaper crowed, 'one of the obstacles being the mental attitude displayed in the inscriptions chalked on a captured pair now lying in a town behind the lines.' (AWM E02877)

An Australian soldier climbs onto *Mephisto*, most likely in the Bois l'Abbé on 23 July 1918 after its salvage. Note the tow cable looped around the Nordenfelt 57mm gun. (AWM P01835.080)

Mephisto's right side adorned with the Australian 'Rising Sun' badge and the 26th Battalion's colour patch. Other signs read: 'Captured by 26th Batt, AIF' and 'Salved by 1st G.C. Coy 5th Bde Tanks.' Note the addition of the AIF rising sun emblem and the crown-wearing British lion, its paw dominating an A7V.

CAPTURED
BY
26TH BATT
A.I.F.
SALVED
BY

CAPTURED BY
AIF
VILLERS BRETONNEUX

Australian soldiers inspect *Mephisto* at the 5th Tank Brigade demonstration ground at Vaux-en-Amienois. Parts from the vehicle scattered on the ground include a fuel tank and radiator. (AWM E02876 & E02935)

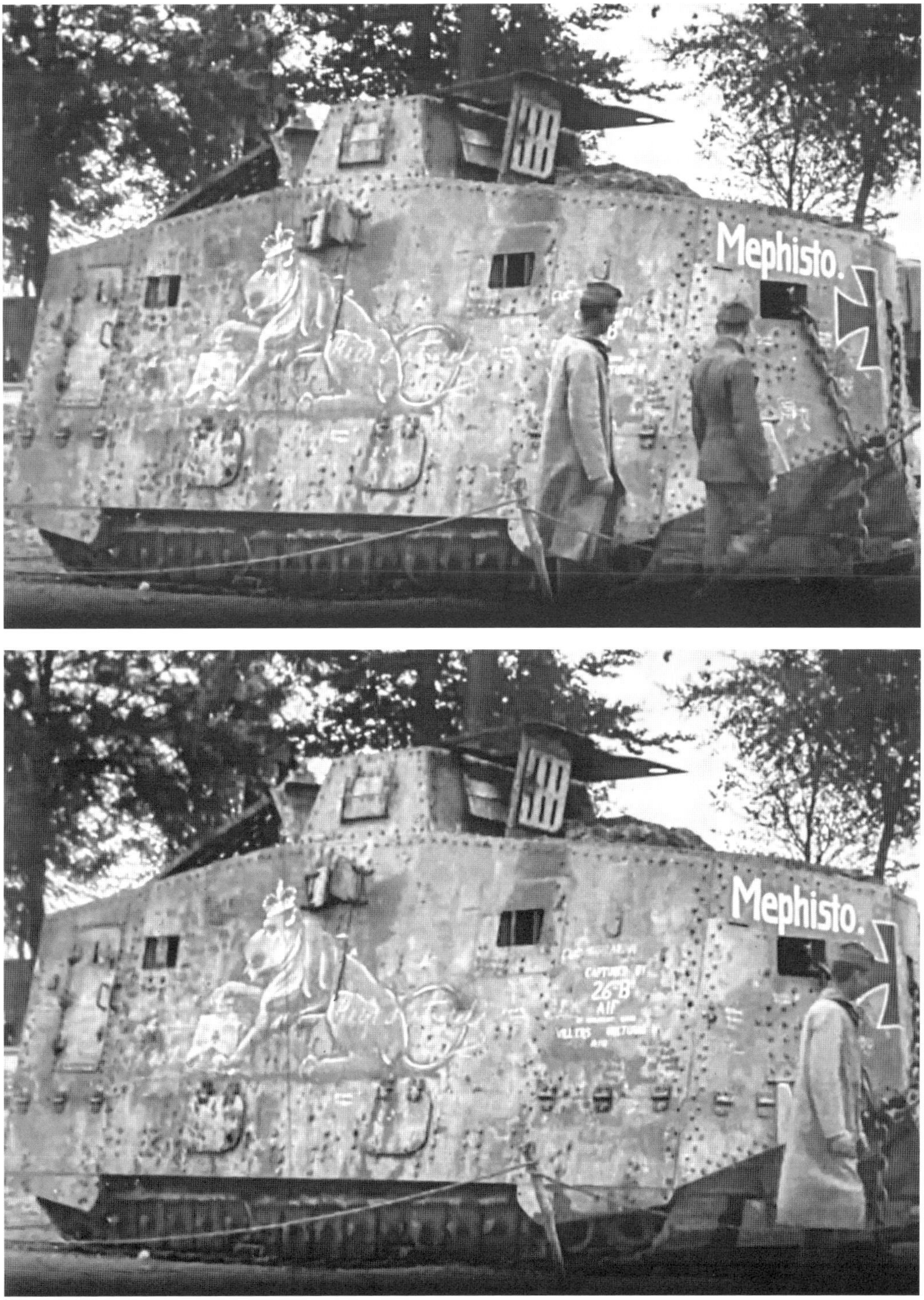

Newsreel stills of *Mephisto* under new ownership, the name newly touched up.

Shipped as a war trophy, *Mephisto* is unloaded from SS *Armagh* onto Norman Wharf, Brisbane, on 14 June 1919.

Mephisto arrives at the Queensland Museum on 23 August 1919, pulled by two Brisbane City Council steamrollers. The tank was originally displayed outdoors. (State Library of Queensland)

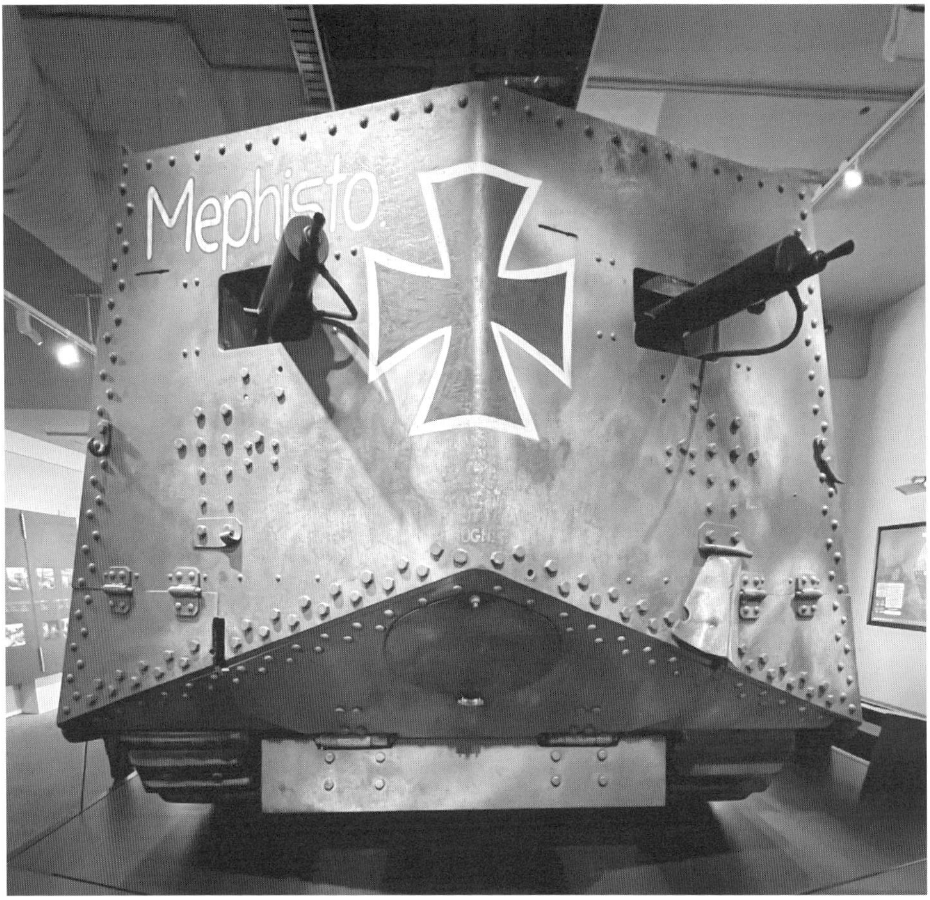

Today, *Mephisto* – the sole surviving A7V – resides at the Queensland Museum, South Bank, as the showpiece in the new Anzac Legacy Gallery.

Hagen and *Schnuck*

Having outdistanced their accompanying infantry, three A7Vs supporting a counter-attack east of Bapaume on 31 August 1918 attempted to re-establish contact. With the appearance of British tanks, however, German artillery opened fire, inadvertently striking 504, *Schnuck*, and 528, *Hagen* – the later slightly damaged, though later ditched; the former heavily hit and likewise abandoned. Recovered by New Zealand troops, both tanks were passed to British authorities. Following Royal Tank Corps investigation, the tanks were exhibited in London. Plans to house them in museums never eventuated and both vehicles were scrapped.

New Zealand troops examine *Schnuck*, 'NZ Division' chalked over the Iron Cross.
(Royal New Zealand Returned and Services' Association)

Allied troops file past *Hagen* while others satisfy their curiosity.

A chalked message on the side reads: 'Captured by 1st Bn, Canterbury Regt; Poor old Bastard; Let me rest in peace.'
(AWM PO3608.025)

Booty. *Hagen* and *Schnuck* arrive at the Tank Corps Headquarters depot at Érin, France.

Hagen with command cupola folded down on a 34-ton railway wagon at the Tanks Corps Central Workshops at Éèrin, France.

Examining *Schnuck*.

Now in London, a policeman stands watch over *Hagen*. Despite protestations from Wellington for the tank to be shipped to New Zealand, it remained in Britain where it was ultimately scrapped.

CAPTURED GERMAN TANK.

Spectators in London clambered on top of the trophy tanks to view the marriage procession to St James' Palace of Princess Patricia of Connaught, daughter of the Duke of Connaught and Commander (later Admiral) Alexander Ramsay on 27 February 1919.

'Swarming over *Hagen*', a newspaper reported, with 'small boys in St James' Park, London, taking possession of a captured German tank.'

Breaking up *Schnuck* in London 1920. The tank's ex-Russian Maxim-Nordenfelt 57mm gun is today displayed at the Imperial War Museum (IWM) North in Manchester.

Nixe II

Abandoned near Brimont, Champagne on 31 May 1918, the French recovered A7V 529, *Nixe II*, presenting it to the US Army in July 1919. Shipped to America, it was examined at the Aberdeen Proving Ground, Maryland, and placed outdoors as an exhibit until 1942 when it was scrapped.

US servicemen photographed with *Nixe II*. (National WWI Museum and Memorial)

Front and rear views of *Nixe II*, stripped of its armament and a large section of frontal armour.
(National WWI Museum and Memorial [top])

Loading *Nixe II* onto a rail wagon. (NARA)

'This photograph', according to a US intelligence report, 'shows the hole cut in the front end of the tank by an acetylene torch for the purpose of removing a gun and pedestal. The shell that pierced the tank in the side burst in the interior and broke and bent various braces. Several shells entered the tank through the top with a similar result.' (NARA)

Damage to *Nixe II* from a shell exploding under the rear of the tank. (NARA)

Close up of the rear shell damage. 'This shows how the armour has been damaged and how the castings and gear cases have been broken, making it very difficult to repair the tank. In several cases it will be necessary to make patterns and have gear casings and castings recast.' (NARA)

'This photograph', the US report documented, 'shows the front view of the power plants, showing how completely the motors have been wrecked. The large casting is the radiator header. All of the radiator sections are missing. The fans, magnetos, carburettor, intake manifolds, push rods, rocker arms, rocker arm brackets, cylinder heads and valves are missing. The valves are of a type unfamiliar to the mechanics of the Proving Ground so far as can be found. All gas leads, connections and ignition systems are completely gone. Other parts which are difficult to identify are also missing. It will be necessary to install two complete American power systems before power could be furnished for the tank.' (NARA)

Rear view of the two engines, minus radiators.

1942. *Nixe II* is towed from the Aberdeen Proving Ground, in Maryland, USA, to be scrapped.

Herkules

Struck by an aerial bomb on 30 August 1918, 562, *Herkules* was, shipped to the BAKP 20 workshop for repairs and later captured by British forces on a rail wagon while en route to its unit. Note the Beutepanzer Mark IV behind it.

527

A7V 527 was trapped in a trench during an attack west of Fort de la Pompelle, Reims, on 1 June 1918. With its clutches burned out from attempts to extricate itself from a trench, the immobilised tank was hit by a French 75-mm shell and abandoned.

'The British invented the tank, and the German authorities have been busy ever since trying to depreciate it', Britain's *Daily Mail* chronicled after the war.

> They needed to. Nothing on the Western Front has so quickly and completely 'put the wind up' the German soldier ... As was to be expected, the German version is a super-tank – at least in appearance. It is bigger, more imposing. uglier, more warlike. In weight and size it must equal a British tank and a half. It seems to have started with the stubborn conviction that only the theory of ours is right. Its alligator tread is more like that of the whippet, with elaborate triple flexible railway-tracks lining it on which run foot-wide wheels. Its armour, double the thickness of ours, is sometimes merely dented before our field guns. Armour-piercing bullets fail to penetrate it, but the inferiority of the metal is

With no threat of capture, 527 remained as a battlefield relic until it was finally scrapped by the French in 1921. (National WWI Museum and Memorial)

evident from the depth of penetration of machine gun bullets. There are, of course, several, improvements readily apparent, though they may be at the sacrifice of more necessary qualities. The entrance is accessible, four feet to the ground-not a back-breaking inconvenience. This is possible from the fact that the interior rests on the running gear, not between the treads. The inside is roomy, consisting of three distinct sections, the fore and aft ones for the guns, the middle one, raised above the compact engines, for the engineer and observer, whose view is through a central cupola. Ventilation is provided by a slat roof, which is bullet-proof. Short ropes, depending from the roof, steady the crew. Fire dangers are minimized by the absence of combustible materials and by asbestos-lined shell boxes, with felt tops to absorb shock and heat. The gunners are seated astride adjustable bicycle seats. The armament varies from three 6-pounders in front and five machine guns behind to six or seven 6-pounders. The general idea has been to develop the characteristics which so terrorise the German-size and ugliness.

Chapter Seven

Mark IV Beutepanzer

Not until March 1918 did Germany's first A7V see combat. As noted earlier, Imperial Germany addressed its armoured shortcoming by reconditioning captured British Mark IV examples to fill the ranks of its fledgling tank force. Many of these tanks were retrieved in the aftermath of the November 1917 fighting around Cambrai or following the 1918 German spring offensive. Colonel Hermann Meyer, from *Chefkraft*, was assigned the task of salvaging the deserted hulks to form Beutepanzer (captured tank) detachments Recovered tanks were shipped by rail to the German BAKP 20, at Charleroi in occupied Belgium.

Unteroffizier Fritz Leu and Leutnant Müller from *Armee-Kraftwagen-Park* 2 (Army Transportation Depot No. 2) or AKP 2, recovered the Mark IV female F13 *Falcon II*. Note the snow on the ground from a storm that battered the front on 7 December 1917.

Seen post recovery, F13 had earlier swerved to avoid a wounded soldier on the ground outside Bourlon, becoming ditched after sliding down a slope. Hopelessly stuck, it was abandoned by its crew. The tank would later feature in a propaganda newsreel.

Recovering F8, *Freemason*, another IV male knocked out at Cambrai. (Bundesarchiv, Bild 104-0941A)

Mark IV male H48 *Hypatia* was knocked out on 23 November 1917 near the main road into Fontaine. Recovered and reconditioned, it served as a Beutepanzer in Abteilung 11.

Unteroffizier Fritz Leu with B8 *Banshee*, a Mark IV female (No. 2556) abandoned by its crew after its engine seized in the fighting for Fontaine. The tank was armed with five Lewis guns, replacing the Vickers and Hotchkiss weapons used in earlier models, which the Germans would modify and retain.

Blarney Castle, B57, a Mark IV female (No. 2873) from the British Army's B Battalion was knocked out near the village of Fontaine-Notre-Dame, west of Cambrai, by a German truck-mounted *Flugabwehrkanone* (aircraft defence cannon or Flak) 7.7cm gun. Note the penetration of the side armour near the port machine gun sponson and dead crew member. Tanks were especially vulnerable when fighting in defended villages.

Right side view of *Blarney Castle*. Mark IV crews were encumbered by the tank's narrow doors in the event of evacuation. Using an improvised charge containing twelve stick grenades against an approaching tank, Reserve Leutnant Dieckmann, 19th Reserve Infantry Regiment, wrote 'that it was thrown forward of the trench against the approaching monster, the left-hand track was torn apart. It could advance no further, being able only to turn in circles. It brought down heavy fire against us and we responded with more made up charges. Just as it was going dark the petrol in the tank exploded and the crew baled out wreathed in flames. We shot them down swiftly. After that we searched the interior and rewarded ourselves by taking everything edible.'

Its hull shattered by Flak projectiles, *Blarney Castle* was broken up for parts needed to maintain a fleet of captured vehicles. (Bundesarchiv, Bild 146-1981-134-31A)

Unusable steel sections from *Blarney Castle* were shipped back to Germany for smelting and reuse. (NARA)

Salvaging the Mark IV female tank B23, *Bandit II*. Lifted onto rollers, the tank, minus sponsons, is towed by a traction engine. Earlier in the fighting, the tank had knocked over a telegraph pole, causing the starboard 6 pounder to become entangled in the telegraph wires. Freeing itself, the tank pressed ahead through the village, where its width proved problematic in the narrow streets. Meeting up with B21 and retiring back to the British lines, the tank was hit three times. The crew bailed out, running under fire to Fontaine where they were captured sheltering in a house. (Bundesarchiv, Bild 146-1982-031-31A)

Mark IV female tank 158 was abandoned after a carburettor fire burnt out the vehicle on 24 November 1917. It is seen here during recovery using a traction engine and rollers. (Bundesarchiv, Bild 104-0959)

German soldiers prepare a captured British Mark IV tank for loading onto a rail wagon. (Bundesarchiv, Bild 104-0958)

Loading C14. (Bundesarchiv, Bild 146-1981-134-23A)

Captured British tanks bound for the BAKP 20 workshops. (Bundesarchiv, Bild 183-P1013-313)

Victorious troops atop Mark IV female 136, minus armament on a Wurttemberg flatbed rail wagon en route to Charleroi.

136 was abandoned by its crew on 24 November 1917 after its engine seized.

Film poster designed by Hans Rudi Erdt for the German silent movie *Die Englischen Tanks bei Cambrai* ('The English Tanks at Cambrai'), which premiered in January 1918. Note the bloodied hand print on the tank hull. Cambrai was celebrated at the time as a heroic example of German military spirit with troops successfully repelling a technically superior army. As General Erich Ludendorff wrote his memoirs, 'The success was the more remarkable because it was in the main achieved by half-tired troops who had not been specially trained for attack … We had won a complete victory over a considerable part of the British Army. It was a good ending to the extremely heavy fighting of 1917.'

Kaiser Wilhelm II inspects captured Mark IV male F13, *Falcon II*, at Bad Kreuznach on 19 December 1917.
(Bundesarchiv, Bild 146-1989-107-33)

Drivers responsible for salvaging enemy tanks are congratulated by the Kaiser. F13 *Falcon II* is seen under camouflage netting in the background.

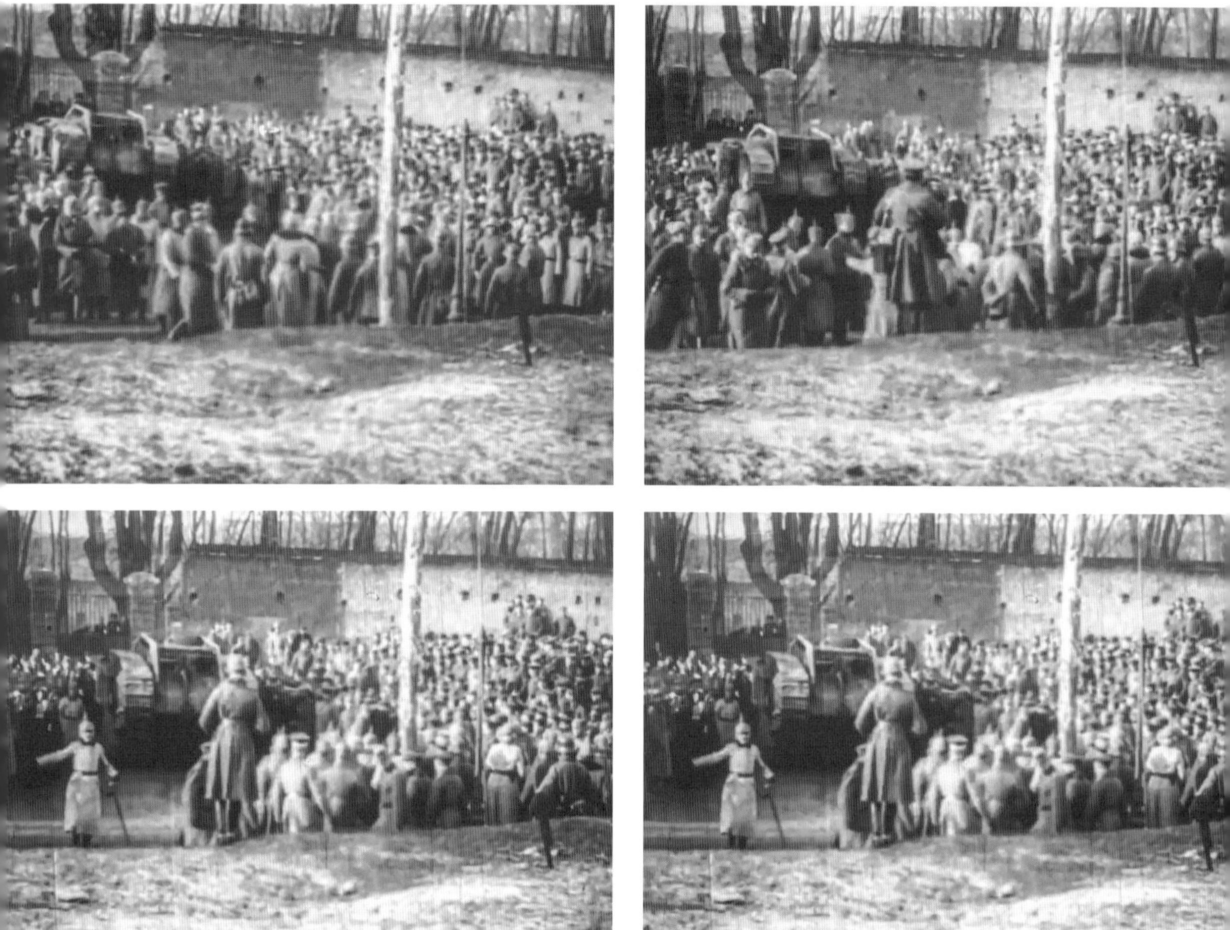

A Mark IV female, likely F13, *Falcon II*, is demonstrated before a large audience of senior officers.

'After the tank battle near Cambrai in December 1917, German drivers drove captured English tanks.'

Stills from *Die Englischen Tanks bei Cambrai* featured F13, *Falcon II*, a female Mark IV, and its ability to push over a large tree. A caption in an English version of the film read: 'German motor troops are learning to handle the captured tanks.'

C14, *Culloden II*, No. 2883, also featured in the film with crew shown exiting the narrow doors of the female variant. The Lewis machine guns have been removed.

Mark IV female C14, No. 2883, *Culloden II*, was recovered at Cambrai after being hit by armour ammunition and catching fire. Under new ownership, the tank is seen here under camouflage netting. Observing a Beutepanzer exercise in early 1918, Ludendorff was less than impressed. 'Our own tank detachments', he wrote postwar, 'suffered heavy losses in the fighting which followed without effecting anything.' (Bundesarchiv, Bild 146-1998-098-10)

Mark IV female H46, *Hyaena* (closest to camera), was one of several tanks lost outside Fontaine-Notre-Dame on 23 November 1917.

Hyaena on display in Munich. A battlefield relic, the tank was exhibited across Germany as a trophy to sell war bonds and was never reconditioned or used as a Beutepanzer.

Hyaena pictured at Leipzig Marktplatz. Note the spudded grousers.

Note the tank's missing port sponson.

German postcard: 'An English tank [F41, *Fray Bentos II*] in Berlin that was captured in the battles near Cambrai'. Photographed in Wittenbergplatz in Berlin's central Schöneberg district during the Winter of 1917/1918. Berlin Press reported paying crowds thronged to see a captured British tank at the Zoological Gardens over Christmastide. The German is a wonderful imitator', British newspapers reported. 'He is now utilising a captured British tank for the purpose of collecting money for war purposes! The tank bank ambles through the streets of Berlin taking in funds just as nonchalantly as if he were doing it in Trafalgar Square or Glasgow.'

Reconditioning a mix of male and female Mark IV tanks inside the large automotive and rail complex at Monceau-sur-Sambre, a Charleroi suburb. BAKP 20 moved to the site, formerly *Société anonyme des ateliers Germain*, between mid-January and 3 February 1918. (NARA)

Another view inside the facility, the workers in the foreground repairing an A7V. (NARA)

Mechanics work on the drive units of former British Mark IV tanks. (NARA)

A refurbished and newly camouflaged Mark IV female bearing the Eisernes Kreuz (Iron Cross) emblem is loaded onto a rail wagon. The colours used are thought to be pre-war Belgian rail – railcar red, green, red-brown, ivory and a clay yellow. A later upgrade of female tanks saw the introduction of two 13mm Tankgewehr anti-tank rifles. (NARA)

Postwar view of the Monceau-sur-Sambre workshops. In addition to German military personnel, the facility employed hundreds of Belgian workers. As the Allies advanced toward Belgium in 1918, the depot was closed with BAKP 20 preparing to relocate to Ginsheim, near Mainz.

Reconditioned Mark IV male tanks were armed with the 5.7cm Maxim-Nordenfelt quick-firing cannon, in place of the QF 6-pounder 6 cwt Hotchkiss gun. A total of 332 shells were carried, usually comprised of 50 percent grapeshot, 20 percent high explosive and 30 percent armour piercing. Further modifications included a compass and cabin escape hatch.

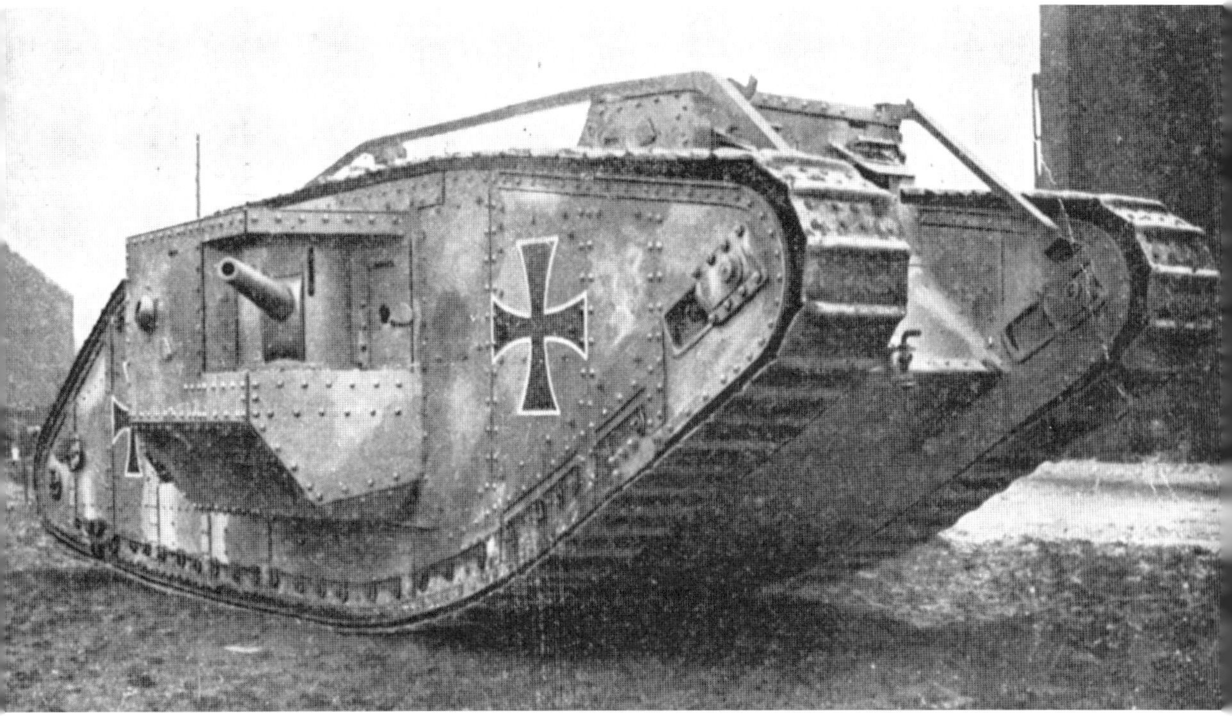

German soldiers, likely tank personnel, pose with a Mark IV female Beutepanzer. After trials to arm reconditioned female variants with heavy MG08 machine guns failed, the tanks were equipped with captured .303 Lewis machine guns, which the *Beute-Maschinengewehr-Instandsetzungs-Werkstatte* (captured machine gun repair workshop) in Brussels rechambered to accept 7.92mm ammunition. (AWM P02882.015)

In addition to utilising captured Mark IV tanks, representatives from Daimler and Krupp visited the BAKP 20 workshops in March 1918 to gauge the feasibility of copying the vehicle. Estimates of 240 tanks produced by June 1919 were provided before the concept was abandoned in June 1918 in favour of producing the Leichter Kampfpanzer.

Mark IV male Beutepanzer, likely the No. 1 tank of Abteilung 11 as denoted by the number within a white ring. With four men needed to steer the ungainly machine, BAKP 20 experimented with a rudimentary system to dispense with the two brakemen, an idea never adopted beyond a single test vehicle.

Western Front, August 1918. German Army troops manhandle guns into position. A Mark IV tank is visible in the background (right). German gunners in 1918 were instructed in the positioning of anti-tank guns: 'In each regimental sector a field gun, with armour-piercing shell, is placed in the outpost zone to fire on tanks. These anti-tank guns, which should have a lateral field of fire, use direct fire. In addition, an anti-tank surveillance battery is placed on both flanks of the division.' (AWM H13398)

Repaired and rebuilt by BAKP 20, this is the No. 1 tank of Abteilung 12.

Chapter Eight

Beutepanzerwagen at War

Whereas the British employed an eight-man crew in a Mark IV tank, the German-manned machines featured a cramped crew of twelve: commander (and brakeman), bow machine gunner, driver, two gearsmen (also acting reserve drivers), four gunners (two for each 5.7cm gun or four machine gunners), mechanic (also a reserve driver) signals NCO, and runner. Like the A7V, each vehicle carried four Gewehr 98 (M98) bolt-action rifles and twenty grenades for dismounted action. 'The British Beutekampfwagen (improved Mk IV)', in Volckheim's estimation,

> had a clearly weaker fighting power than the A7V. Due to the exposed tracks and the weaker armour protection, the tank was vulnerable to infantry fire. Driver and commander were placed in the front of the vehicle. While the driver operated the engine and the transmission, the commander had to handle the steering brakes to initiate turns ... Orders were shouted. The commander had no influence on the firing of the weapons; he was occupied guiding the tank by operating the steering brakes. The commander's observation was limited; he had no view to the sides ... Despite the many disadvantages of the Beutekampfwagen we had been able to gain many great successes. These positive results were gained owing to the abilities of the commanders and the competence of the crews rather than to the technical perfection of the [British] tanks.

Reconditioned Mark IV tanks was assigned to six Sturmpanzer Kraftwagen Abteilungen Nos 11–16, renamed Schwere Kampfwagen-Abteilungen (Beute) on 2 October 1918. The nominal strength of each Abteilung was five Beutepanzer – three female and two male tanks.

Mark IV male aboard a rail wagon. A British tanker recalled the peril of the loading procedure. 'They are driven on and off the train under their own power, but this performance requires care, skill, and experience. A Mark I or a Mark IV tank is not too easy to steer, while the space between the track and the edge of the truck is alarmingly small … I remember that the entraining was poor. We took nearly forty minutes. Entraining and detraining provide searching tests of a tank's mechanical efficiency and the skill of a crew. If there is any flaw in the tuning, any clumsiness in the driver, driving on to a train will discover it. A tank dislikes a train. It slides on with grunts of obstinate dissatisfaction.' (AWM H11819)

Stills from a German newsreel of a Beutepanzer Mark IV female pair (the leading tank is *Greta*, is from Abteilung 14) in mid-July 1918 during the Second Battle of Marne. Due to the smaller crew size of the British Mark IV, Beute Abteilungen had a lower number of personnel compared to their A7V equivalents with seven officers, thirty-six non-commissioned officers and ninety-nine enlisted men. Each Abteilung contained five Mark IVs, three cars and eight trucks.

Newsreel footage of the Beutepanzer Mark IV female, *ERNI*, No. 3 tank of Abteilung 12. This tank later served with Freikorps during the 1919 uprising.

Mark IV male under netting at Wavrin, in northern France, in readiness for an attack on 9 April 1918. The German public read of captured British tanks in service in June 1918: 'Now, with German crews, they could show what the tank arm, under skilful leadership, could achieve. Now, the young storm troop leaders, who so often, at the Somme, Arras and Cambrai had stood in the path of the fire-spitting tank fleets until they were destroyed by German artillery, could now – as tank commanders – carry terror and fear into the ranks of the English infantry.'

(**Above**) Curious infantry watch as tank crew adjust grouser track extensions. The rails on the British tanks were modified to allow the unditching beam to pass over the tank without hitting the newly installed compass housing.

(**Opposite, above**) A Mark IV female is passed by a 3-ton Benz KL14 truck in Armentières after Abteilung 11's combat debut near St Quentin. Unteroffizier Fritz Bayerer (in Wagen 218) wrote of the strain of fighting after Anglo-US troops pushed through the Hindenburg Line in October: 'The sweat was flowing in streams mixing with the smoke of the guns. As we had to aim and fire the guns, it was difficult to remain seated on the tiny bicycle saddle and whenever we went over rough terrain we used to fall off. With our bare hands, we had to clean the puddles that were the result of oil cans that had fallen to the floor which was littered with empty shell cases. We wiped the sweat from our eyes with oil, water and slimy gunpowder forming a layer of glistening colours on our faces and uniforms … our fighting capabilities suffered from extensive sweating, especially when sweat splashed on the optics of the scope. This targeting device left much to be desired as its field of vision was much too small.' (NARA)

(**Opposite, below**) Muddy Mark IV female under camouflage netting. Too few Mark IV Beutepanzers limited operations to piecemeal attacks, such as their participation on 9 July 1918 in an offensive against French forces ensconced along the Matz River. Of the seven tanks assigned to the operation, two broke down prior to the assault, leaving five vehicles to support two infantry divisions. In comparison, the French Army employed 478 Renault FT tanks the previous month in an attack on German lines. J.F.C. Fuller noted some later success, by the Germans, writing: 'On 8 October, some fifteen captured British machines were used against us in the Cambrai sector. Of this action the German account states that these tanks were employed defensively to fill up a gap in their line; whether this was so or not, they undoubtedly produced a demoralising effect amongst our own men, equilibrium only being re-established when two of them were put out of action.'

203

Mark IV female *Liesel*. The slow moving British machines were unable to keep pace with swiftly advancing Stoß-truppen (shock troops). Hauptman Willy Rohr of Sturmbataillon 5 (Rohr) complained that the 'captured English tanks have shown less combat value than German tanks. Any cooperation with the infantry appears to be impossible because of the modest speed.'

Mark IV male *Fritz* prepares to drag *Liesel* (less unditching beam) from an anti-tank ditch. Both tanks belonged to Abteilung No. 14, which became operational under Hauptmann Wilhelm Negenborn on 7 May 1918.

Broken down Beutepanzers were rarely recovered from the battlefield, instead being replaced by a newly refurbished vehicle. Note the iron cross emblem on the escape hatch.

The crew of the Mark IV male Beutepanzer, *Heinz*, Wagen 207 and the No. 4 tank of Abteilung 14, and commander, Leutnant Heinrich Köhler. J.F.C. Fuller believed the 'moral [*sic*] of the German Tank Corps was not high, and as regards the personnel of the captured Mark IV Tanks it was decidedly low, the Germans having made considerable efforts to prove to their own troops, that this type of tank was both vulnerable and ineffective.'

Heinz was lost in action near Fort de la Pompelle, southeast of Reims, on 1 June 1918.

143. LA POMPELLE — Attaque allemande du 15 Juillet 1918 — Le tank Heinz est resté en panne au bord de la tranchée allemande qu'il n'a pu traverser — Broken down tank.

After the battle. Lieutenant Colonel Clarence Benjamin Francisco, US Medical Officer, assigned to 1st, 32nd, and 35th Division in France, with his wife and another woman behind the derelict *Heinz*. (National WWI Museum and Memorial)

Abandoned Mark IV female, *HEDDA*, Wagen 102, a tank originally assigned to Abteilung 11, under Hauptmann Adolf Reinhard Koch. The detachment first saw combat on 21 March during Operation *Michael*. *HEDDA* was subsequently transferred to Abteilung 13 in late May 1918. Unteroffizier Karl Schreyer, Abteilung 11, a Lewis gunner, recounted a later assault: 'Our tank advanced further, tipped headlong into a trench, pulled itself out again and headed towards the Aisne [River]. Then, all of a sudden, it started. We were met by raging machine gun fire getting more intense by the second. After closing the hatches, I trained my gun on an enemy nest and let fly with everything I had. When I had emptied the first drum magazine, felt a sudden blow. My gun had taken a hit and became useless. A bullet ricocheted on the spring housing, before falling to the floor. Quickly, we installed the spare gun which soon shared the same fate of its predecessor. This time a bullet had hit the barrel from the outside and blocked it. In this situation, our unarmoured guns were quite useless. The machine gunners in the German A7V tanks were far better off.'

Male Beutepanzer *Moritz*, Wagen 206 from Abteilung 11, was abandoned on 1 June 1918 near Fort de la Pompelle after its engine overheated. With German infantry in retreat, the tank was blown up by three of its crew including Josef 'Sepp' Dietrich.

Max, a Mark IV male was assigned to Abteilung 13 as Wagen 201. The Bavarian formation first saw combat near Juvincourt, northern France, on 27 May 1918. *Max* was lost in action on 1 June 1918 at Fort de La Pompelle, west of Reims. The inexperienced crew had failed to secure the tank's sponsons after unloading from a rail car. Vibrations that followed shattered the differential gear. No attempt was made to recover the tank.
(Nicolas Joseph Gustave Crouvezier / Archives municipales de Nancy & National WWI Museum and Memorial)

Tourists in uniform. Missing its main armament, a soldier in the left sponson poses with a 5.7cm shell. Numerous chalk crosses mark points where projectiles had penetrated the hull. *(National WWI Museum and Memorial)*

Max's graffitied Eisernes Kreuz symbol altered to depict the German military decoration, bearing the dates 1914, 1918 and 'W' for Kaiser Wilhelm II. (National WWI Museum and Memorial)

Mark IV female *Ännchen*, Wagen 107, the No. 5 tank of Abteilung 12, was approaching Fort de la Pompelle (during the Second Battle of the Marne) when it fell under accurate artillery fire directed by a spotter plane. Abandoning the tank, the crew used three of its Lewis guns help to repel a French counterattack.

Mark IV female *Dora,* Wagen 128 of Abteilung 14. Note the driver's hatch, a BAKP 20 modification.

Mark IV female *Lotte* was Abteilung 14, was also lost during the fighting against French forces at Fort de La Pompelle on 15 July 1918. Although waxed cotton was used to dampen noise inside the tank, a Beutepanzer gunner likened the noise to wearing a large 'bucket over your head, from which the outside is relentlessly tormented with the blows of several hammers. Someone then inserts a pistol into the inside of the bucket and fires it several times.'

Lotte became a popular postwar tourist attraction and postcard subject.

Staff Nurse Dorothy Sevilla White, Australian Army Nursing Service, photographed next to *Lotte*. (AWM P03253.002)

French postcards of *Liesel*, Wagen 113, Abteilung 14, at Fort de La Pompelle. (National WWI Museum and Memorial)

Precipitously balanced, the tank was listed as a battlefield relic in the 1925 Michelin touring guide. Subsequently removed by concerned French authorities, it was replaced by a British tank depicted as L52, *Lyric*, for tourists wishing to see a war relic in-situ.

(National WWI Museum and Memorial)

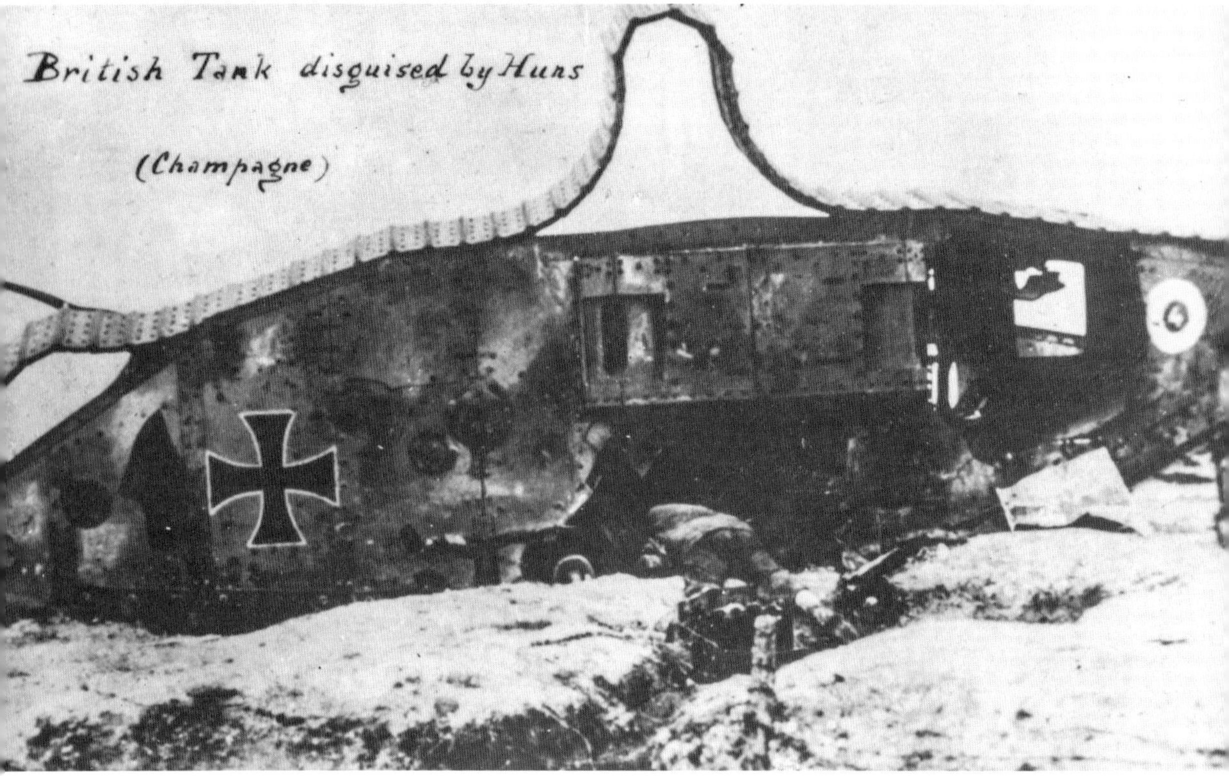

Mark IV female No. 4 of Abteilung 11 was blown up by retreating German troops in September or early October 1918.

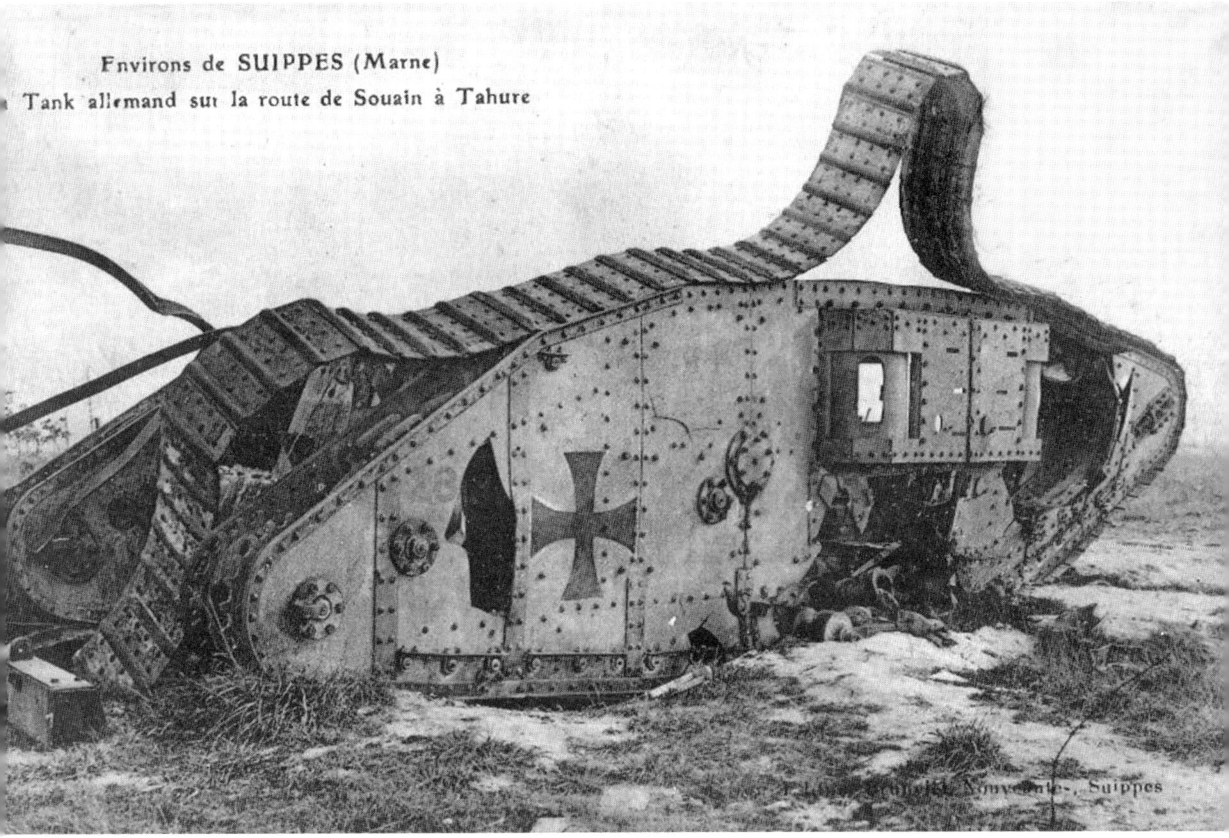

Frontal view of the destroyed Beutepanzer.

A Mark IV female, with insignia hidden by mud, negotiates a trench during a trial run. (AWM H13463 & H13462)

Back in Allied hands, a female Beutepanzer bears a chalked message: 'recaptured by the 6th Labour Company, Middlesex Regiment.' (AWM P00520.003)

Another recaptured female Beutepanzer (minus name or number), this time seized by the Sherwood Foresters in February 1918. Note the later style, straight-armed Balkenkreuz emblem. From early May 1918, British tanks carried large white-red-white strips on their forward sides and roof to distinguished them from German-operated Mark IVs. Note the open escape hatch, raised unditching beam rails and marking. (Alexander Turnbull Library)

New Zealand troops (Canterbury Regiment) examine a recaptured Mark IV female also bearing the later-style Balkenkreuz insignia.

'Indifferent as were the German tank tactics as compared with our own', J.F.C. Fuller asserted, 'one fact was most striking, this being that the British infantry no more than the German would or could withstand a tank attack. The reason for this is a simple one, namely, inability to do so. So pronounced was this feeling of helplessness that when, during our own retirement in March 1918, rumours were afloat that German tanks were approaching, our men in several sectors of the line broke and fell back. During the German retirement a few months later on we find exactly the same lowering of moral by self-suggested fear, fear based on the inability to overcome the danger. This moral effect produced by the tank was appreciated by the Germans, for in a note issued by the XVIIth German Army we find: "Our own tanks strengthen the moral of the infantry to a tremendous extent, even if employed only in small numbers, and experience has shown that they have a considerable demoralising effect on the hostile infantry."'

On 1 November 1918, five Beutepanzer were ordered to repulse an Allied counterattack. It was an inauspicious final act. Only three of the five tanks moved off with the infantry; two were soon knocked out by artillery; the lagging last machine never saw combat. (National WWI Museum and Memorial)

Mark A Whippet Tanks

As well as Mark IV tanks, a number of Mark A Whippet tanks were also captured, two of which were restored to running order by BAKP 20 mechanics. These tanks fell victim to the German Second Army – '*Erobert von der II Armee*'. (AWM P00098.002 (top))

Captured Whippet (left) and Mark IV tanks. The 14-ton medium Mark A, or Whippet, was designed in 1917 by William Tritton of Fosters. The lightly armoured tank had a top speed of 8mph (13km/h). Armed with three or four Hotchkiss .303 machine guns, it had a crew of four – commander, driver and two machine gunners. (National WWI Museum and Memorial)

The Whippet first appeared on the battlefield in March 1918 during the German spring offensive. Although intended to exploit breakthrough situations, it found some success in a defensive role, stalling a push on the Somme that month and later charging two German battalions on 24 April 1918, causing heavy casualties.

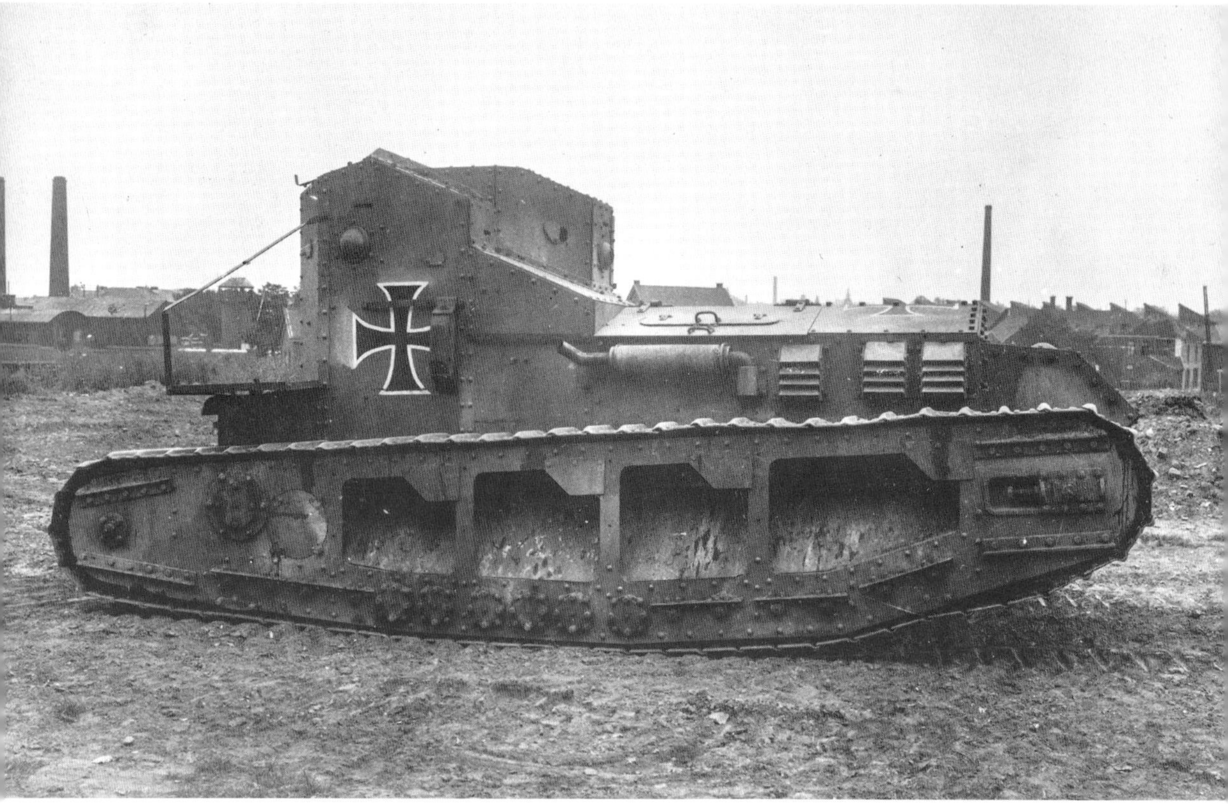

Captured Whippet photographed at Monceau-sur-Sambre, August 1918. It was a difficult vehicle to drive with each of the two 45hp Tylor engines having its own clutch and gearbox. On turning the steering wheel, directly connected to the throttle levers, one engine sped up while the other slowed. In practice it was easy to stall one or both engines. Steering was also assisted by braking.

One of the two operational Beutepanzer Whippets, now featuring the characteristic BAKP 20 camouflage.

Trialling a Whippet at the BAKP 20 proving ground. As fast as the A7V, the tank could surmount obstacles up to 80cm high. (NARA)

French Tanks

French tanks were also captured and evaluated. This poor quality photograph shows a French-supplied, US Renault FT that was captured by Willy Rohr's Sturmbataillon 5 in 1918.

The Renault FT *Hargneuse III*, with mock turret, sandwiched between Abteilung 14 machines *Heinz* and *Liesel*. (NARA)

A small number of captured French tanks were unofficially pressed into service. This Saint-Chamond was purportedly used against the US 1st Infantry Division in July 1918.

Dummy Tanks

Dummy tanks, superficially resembling British and French vehicles, were commonly used by the Germans for training purposes. A report filed after an eight-day anti-tank instruction course in January 1918 recorded: 'Wooden tanks were used, at which machine guns and trench mortars fired until the tanks had penetrated beyond the second line, when the defense was taken over by the artillery. Instruction in the vulnerable parts of the tank was given.' A later document (dated 13 September 1918) following exercises involving Minenwerfer trench mortars firing on tank silhouettes, concluded that the effective range was 200 to 600 metres. 'The use of wooden tank silhouettes', it highlighted, was 'necessary during target practice, and they are drawn by a wire cable at a speed that simulates that of real tanks.'

View of a detailed wooden Renault FT tank replica on wheels found at Charleroi. (AWM E04444)

Wooden FT abandoned by German forces. Note the detailed painted exhaust. German soldiers were taught that 'tanks are dangerous for the infantry only at very close range (less than 100 metres), on account of the inaccuracy of their fire. Beyond this distance excellent results can be obtained with anti-tank rifles, machine guns and concentrated charges.' (NARA)

Australian soldiers beside three dummy Renault FT tanks. This revolutionary French design was more manoeuvrable and harder to hit than the preceding heavier French designs. (AWM E05255)

Crude representation of a British tank made from reeds.

Wooden mock-up of a Mark IV female, at Pontfaverges, today Pontfaverger-Moronvilliers, in north-eastern France. In response to a tank assault, German troops in 1918 were instructed to form 'anti-tank groups'. 'In the forward battle zone, anti-tank groups, under especially energetic leaders, are to be formed. These will consist of anti-tank guns, machine guns, anti-tank rifles and trench mortars. The various weapons of these groups need not be close together, but they must be able to render mutual support within their group, except in the case of anti-tank rifles, which must be in groups of four to six. Groups are to be distributed in depth in the battle zone.' Tanks, the defenders learnt, 'are best attacked from the rear.' (NARA)

US Soldiers retrieve a wooden Whippet replica with the aid of a Ford truck.

Chapter Nine

Post War

Following the abdication and flight of Kaiser Wilhelm II to the Netherlands on 8 November 1918, *Spartakusbund* (Spartacus League) revolutionaries contested the new Weimar Government led by Friedrich Ebert's Social Democratic Party. Ebert, Germany's first chancellor, actively suppressed the armed uprising using the right-wing Freikorps ('Free Corps'), former Imperial soldiers (that in time developed strong ties with the budding Nazi Party and Sturmabteilung). A small number of armoured vehicles still in German hands after the November 1918 Armistice were used to quell uprisings in Berlin, Munich and Leipzig. Beginning as *Tank-Abteilung Körting*, under Hauptmann Georg Körting, the diminutive armoured force became *Kommando der Kampfwagenabteilungen*, or Kokampf, before reverting to direct army control as *Army Freiwilligen-Panzer-Kraftwagen-Abteilung*. Kokampf armour included two A7V communications tanks reconfigured as riot control tanks, an A7V (possibly 507), a Whippet, several Mark IV tanks plus several armoured cars.

Kokampf armoured cars in Berlin. The sign reads: 'Take care stay in your houses. In the streets danger to life because we are shooting.' Note the use of Totenkopf insignia.

Improvised armoured car built on the chassis of an American Packard 3-ton truck captured from Russian forces in 1917 in the town of Dvinsk (now Daugavpils in Latvia).

Makeshift armoured truck, an *Armee-Lastwagen* of Loeb-Werke AG, in Berlin during the Kapp Putsch of March 1920, an attempted coup to overthrow the Weimar Republic. (Bundesarchiv, Bild 146-1972-033-17)

Two Kokampf tanks at Berlin-Tempelhof, January 1919. It is believed that two Funkpanzer, mobile communications tanks, were completed after the war by Steffens & Nölle as riot control tanks. One became *Hedi*, the other '54'. Note the distinctive command 'domes' in place of the larger cupola installed on wartime A7V tanks.

The first of three images of tank '54' displaying allegiance to the government with the slogan *Panzer-Kampfwagen-Abteilung Regierungs-Treue-Truppen* (Panzer-Kampfwagen-Division Government Loyalty Troops).

Panzer-Kraftwagen-Abteilung
Regierungs-treue-Truppen
54

Panzer-Kraftwagen-Abteilung
Regierungs-treue-Truppen
54

Hedi, a second Kokampf A7V, was deployed at Leipzig in May 1919.

Skirmish in Bülowplatz square (today Rosa-Luxemburg-Platz). The Kokampf Mark IV female is towing a 7.7cm Feldkanone. (AWM, A01305)

The Mark IV female *Hanni*, formerly the No. 4 tank of Abteilung 12, was one of several Kokampf Mark IV tanks deployed against the communists. Curiously, the vehicle at the time was referred to as a 'Tankwagen'.

MANN
Waren
ewaren.
Parlie
Waren

Große Straßenkämpfe in Berlin während des Generalstreiks.
Erstürmter spartakistischer Schützengraben in Lichtenberg.
S.&G.S.i.B.
Ø №46.

Freikorps troops armed with rifles and *Stielhandgranate* ('stick hand grenade') stand before *Hanni*.

Running repairs for the second captured Whippet, which became '53', seen here outside the Eden Hotel in Berlin on the Kurfürstendamm, today Budapester Straße. The hotel gained notoriety in 1919 because of its connection with the arrest and murder of Marxist revolutionaries Karl Liebknecht and Rosa Luxemburg.

(**Above**) The same Whippet photographed in a Berlin. (AWM H06815)

(**Opposite**) Under the oxyacetylene torch. Article 171 of the Treaty of Versailles forbade Germany from possessing tanks. Propaganda was duly circulated showing compliant workers dismantling Freikorps armour: 'Disarmament is the first perquisite for solving the world crisis! The work of the Disarmament Conference does not seem to lead to any goal, as France is not willing to base its own disarmament on the disarmament provisions of the Versailles Treaty, which Germany has fully implemented. Our picture shows the destruction of German tanks in 1919.' The lower image shows the breaking up of *Hanni*.

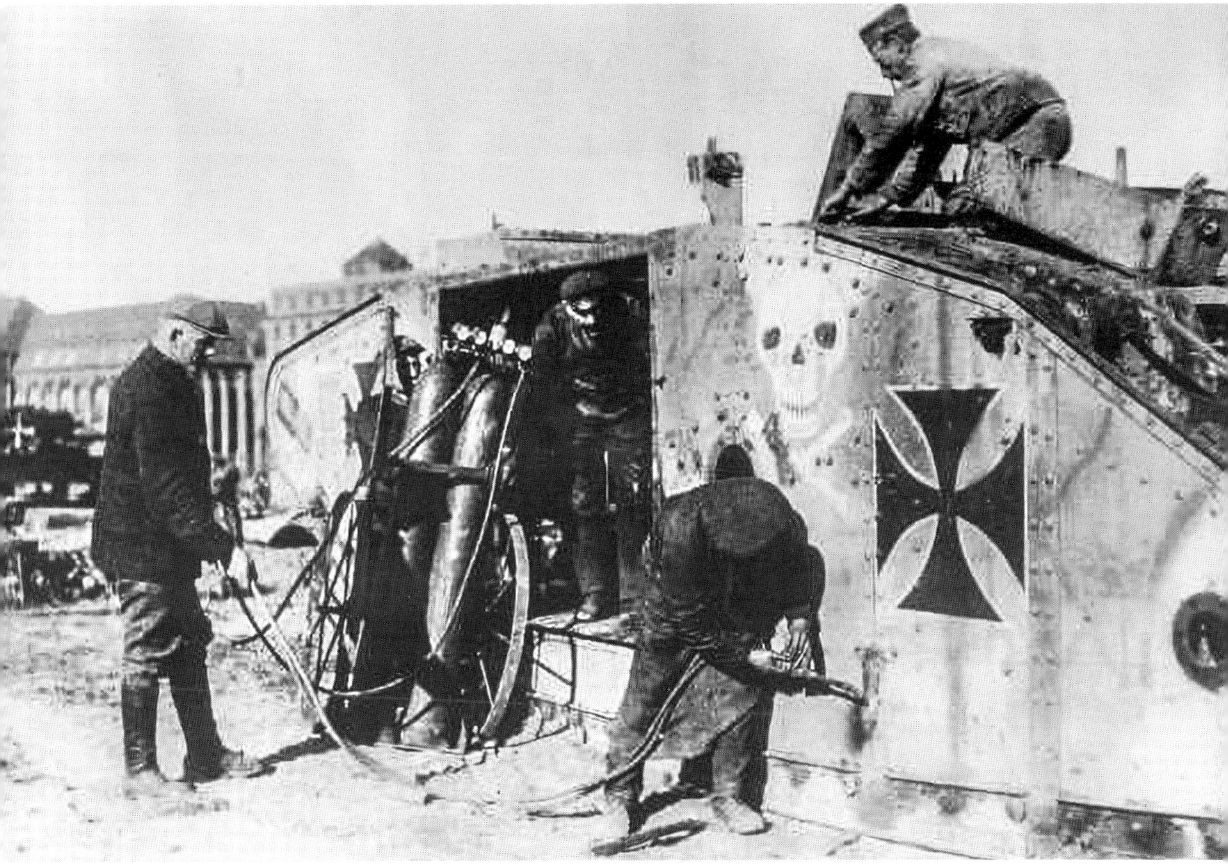

Early Nazi propaganda. *Stoßtrupp 1917* ('Shock Troop 1917') was a 1934 war film written and directed by Nazi party member and propagandist Hans Zöberlein. Based on his nationalistic 1931 book, *Der Glaube an Deutschland* (*Faith in Germany*), which included a foreword by Adolf Hitler, the film depicts stormtroopers fighting on the Western Front during the First World War.

A scene from *Stoßtrupp 1917* portraying a British armoured attack with a (mock-up) Mark V hermaphrodite.

While Heinz Guderian is often viewed as the mastermind behind Nazi Germany's armoured force and the architect of the Blitzkrieg concept, other lesser-known proponents included Fritz Heigl, Wilhelm Brandt, Werner von Fritsich, Alfred von Vollard-Bockelberg, Oswald Lutz and Ernst Volckheim. The latter became a prolific author on armoured theory and tactics – reinforced by his wartime A7V experience – during the 1920s and 1930s. Seriously wounded in October 1918, Volckheim was retained in General Hans von Seeckt's (Chief of the German General Staff) 100,000-strong Reichswehr. Assigned to the Inspectorate of Motor Transport in the Defense Ministry, in 1925 he taught armoured warfare and motorized tactics at the Infantry School at Döberitz, in eastern Germany. His 1922 pamphlet *Der Kampfwagen der Zukunft* ('The Combat Vehicle of the Future') was followed by a well-received book, the (aforementioned) 1923 *Die deutschen Kampfwagen im Weltkriege*. Aside from dozens of articles on armoured warfare, he proposed the formation of light armoured battalions paired with infantry at company level as a breakthrough tactic in his 1924 *Die Kampfwagen in der heutigen Kriegsführung* ('The Tank in Today's Warfare'), a standard Reichswehr text.

Volckheim's *Die Kampfwagen in der heutigen Kriegsführung* outlined vulnerable points on the British Mark IV tank.

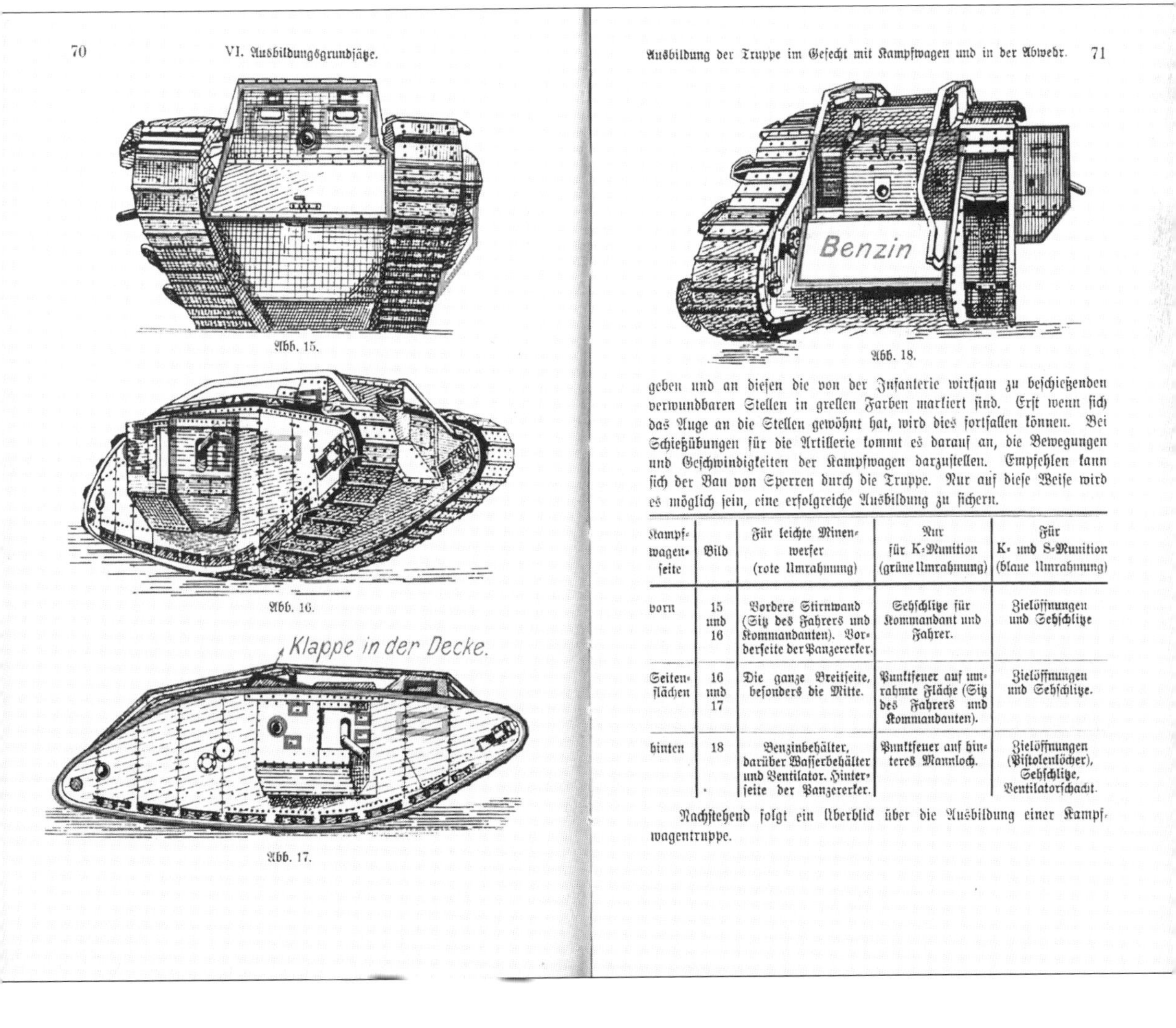

70 VI. Ausbildungsgrundsätze.

Abb. 15.

Abb. 16.

Klappe in der Decke.

Abb. 17.

Ausbildung der Truppe im Gefecht mit Kampfwagen und in der Abwehr. 71

Benzin

Abb. 18.

geben und an diesen die von der Infanterie wirksam zu beschießenden verwundbaren Stellen in grellen Farben markiert sind. Erst wenn sich das Auge an die Stellen gewöhnt hat, wird dies fortfallen können. Bei Schießübungen für die Artillerie kommt es darauf an, die Bewegungen und Geschwindigkeiten der Kampfwagen darzustellen. Empfehlen kann sich der Bau von Sperren durch die Truppe. Nur auf diese Weise wird es möglich sein, eine erfolgreiche Ausbildung zu sichern.

Kampfwagenseite	Bild	Für leichte Minenwerfer (rote Umrahmung)	Nur für K-Munition (grüne Umrahmung)	Für K- und S-Munition (blaue Umrahmung)
vorn	15 und 16	Vordere Stirnwand (Sitz des Fahrers und Kommandanten). Vorderseite der Panzererker.	Sehschlitze für Kommandant und Fahrer.	Zielöffnungen und Sehschlitze
Seitenflächen	16 und 17	Die ganze Breitseite, besonders die Mitte.	Punktfeuer auf umrahmte Fläche (Sitz des Fahrers und Kommandanten).	Zielöffnungen und Sehschlitze.
hinten	18	Benzinbehälter, darüber Wasserbehälter und Ventilator. Hinterseite der Panzererker.	Punktfeuer auf hinteres Mannloch.	Zielöffnungen (Pistolenlöcher), Sehschlitze, Ventilatorschacht.

Nachstehend folgt ein Überblick über die Ausbildung einer Kampfwagentruppe.

Volckheim believed that the Germany army had underestimated the tank during the war. He foresaw the tank's role in mobile warfare – heavy tanks, faster than the A7V and with a wider radius of action, would overcome obstacles, fight independently or assist infantry; fast light tanks armed with machine guns could reach 60km/h in tactical reconnaissance, working in conjunction with cavalry and infantry. Heavy tanks would be deployed in three waves – the first would smash through enemy lines and neutralise strongpoints; the second would destroy artillery and machine guns targeting the first echelon; the third wave would assist infantry to advance.

Guderian later made a passing reference to Volckheim in his memoirs, recalling him to be:

> … engaged in collating information concerning the very limited use of German armoured vehicles, and the incomparably greater employment of enemy tank forces during the war … though weak in theory it gave me something to go on.'

An overly fast Mark IV mock-up, No. 7, based on an automobile chassis featured in the Karl Ritter film *Unternehmen Michael* ('Operation Michael'). The film premièred on 7 September 1937 during the 9th Nazi Party rally at the Ufa-Palast in Nuremberg and in Berlin at the Ufa-Palast am Zoo on 19 November 1937.

Interwar A7V memorial erected by the Cambrai Barracks, Panzer-Regiment 5, Wünsdorf. A brass plaque read: 'In the Spirit of Comrades from the World War: Attack–Fight–Win.' Panzer-Regiment 5 later participated in the campaigns against Poland and France before deployment to North Africa in February 1941. It ceased to exist after the defeat of the Axis forces in Tunisia in May 1943.

Oberstleutnant Ernst Volckheim, veteran of Villers-Bretonneux and now commander of Panzer-Abteilung z.b.V. 40, salutes an armoured parade outside the University of Oslo, Norway, on 1 October 1940. Prominent on his black Panzer uniform is the Imperial Tank Badge. (National Archives of Norway)

Oberstleutnant Ernst Volckheim (right) beside Generaloberst Nikolaus von Falkenhorst (saluting), *Wehrmachtsbefehlshaber des besetzten Norwegen*, commander of German troops in Norway 1940 to 1944, and his aide-de-camp, Kurt Treuhaupt.

Another A7V veteran, SS-Obergruppenführer Josef 'Sepp' Dietrich, seen here with his with his second wife Ursula, likewise wears the Imperial Tank Badge. Dietrich, remembered for his role in the January 1945 Malmedy massacre during the Battle of Bulge, had risen to lead the 6th Panzer Army by the end of the Second World War.
(Bundesarchiv, Bild 101III-Alber-045-30 / Alber, Kurt)

In a remarkable coda, Allied troops discovered two wrecked Mark V tanks in Berlin – a Mark V hermaphrodite or composite, and a Mark V female – in 1945. Previously displayed in Smolensk, Russia, as monuments to the Russian Civil War, the tanks were brought to Germany after Hitler invaded the Soviet Union in June 1941. Whether they played any role in the defense of Berlin in 1945 is a source of ongoing conjecture.

Bibliography

Australian War Memorial (AWM)

AWM 3DRL/2316 General Sir John Monash, Personal Files Book 15, 10 June–31 July 1917.

AWM 27 310/75 [Conduct of Operations:] Translation of captured German Order – Organisation of anti-tank defence (July 1918).

AWM 3DRL/5023 Auto Diary of Charles Malcolm Smith, 1918–1919.

US Army

United States Army, *Summary of Information: Second Section. General Staff. General Headquarters, American Expeditionary Forces. 1918–05.*

United States Army Armor School, *Armor in Battle*, Leadership Branch, Leadership and Training Division, Command and Staff Department (Fort Knox, 1986).

United States War Department, *A Survey of German Tactics, 1918* (Washington, DC, 1918).

During, F. (ed.), 'Review of Military Literature', *The Command and General Staff School Quarterly*, March 1937, Vol. XVII, No. 64.

Published Sources

Albrecht, W., *Gunther Burstyn (1879–1945) und die Entwicklung der Panzerwaffe* (Osnabrück, 1973).

Anderson, T., *The History of the Panzerwaffe, Vol. 1: 1939–1942* (Oxford, 2015).

Cooper, B., *The Ironclads of Cambrai* (Barnsley, 2002)

——, *Tank Battles of World War I* (Barnsley, 2014).

Fletcher, D. (ed.), *Tanks and Trenches: First Hand Accounts of Tank Warfare in the First World War* (London, 1996).

——, *The British Tanks 1915–19* (Ramsbury, 2001).

——, *British Battle Tanks World War I to 1939* (Oxford, 2016).

——, *British Mark IV Tank* (New York, 2012).

——, *Medium Mark A Whippet* (New York, 2014).

Foley, J., *A7V Sturmpanzerwagen* (Surrey, 1967).

Fuller, J.F.C., *Tanks In The Great War 1914–1918* (New York, 1920).

Guderian, H., *Panzer Leader* (London, 1950).

Habeck, M.R., *Storm of Steel: The Development of Armor Doctrine in Germany and the Soviet Union, 1919–1939* (New York, 2003).

Horman, J.M., *Uniforms of the Panzer Troops: 1917 To The Present* (West Chester, PA, 1989).

Hundleby, M. & R. Strasheim, *The German A7V Tank and the Captured British Tanks of World War I* (Sparkford, 1990).

——, *Sturmpanzer A7V: First of the Panzers* (Erlangen, 2020).

Icks, R.J., *Famous Tank Battles* (New York, 1972).

Jones, R.E., Rarey, G.H. and Icks R.J., *The Fighting Tanks Since 1916* (Washington, DC, 1933).
Junger, E., *Storm of Steel* (New York, 1961).
Kendall, P., *Bullecourt 1917: Breaching the Hindenburg Line* (Stroud, 2017).
Koch, F., *Beutepanzer im Ersten Weltkrieg* (Frieburg, 1994).
Langford, W., *Somme Intelligence Fourth Army HQ 1916* (Barnsley, 2013).
Ludendorff, Erich von, *My War Memories* (London, 1919).
Lloyd George, David, *War Memoirs of David Lloyd George* (London, 1938).
Ludendorff, E., *Ludendorff's Own Story*, Vol. 11 (New York, 1919).
Macksey, K., *The Tank Pioneers* (London, 1981).
Macksey, K. and M. Kaye, *Tank Warfare: A History of Tanks in Battle* (New York, 1972).
Martin, D.E., *Londoners on the Western Front: The 58th (2/1st London) Division in the Great War* (Barnsley, 2014).
Millett, A. and W. Murray (eds), *The Dynamics of Necessity: German Military Policy during the First World War, Military Effectiveness, Vol. 1: The First World War* (London, 1988).
Mitcham, S.W., *The Panzer Legions: A Guide to the German Army Tank Divisions of WWII and Their Commanders* (Mechanicsburg, 2007).
Moore, C., *Tank Hunter: World War One* (Stroud, 2017).
Nash, D.B., *Imperial German Army Handbook 1914–1918* (London, 1980).
Pidgeon, T., *The Tanks at Flers: An Account of the First Use of Tanks in War at the Battle of Flers-Courcelette, the Somme, 15 September 1916* (Cobham, 1995).
——, *Fleurs & Gueudecourt* (Barnsley, 2002).
——, *Tanks On The Somme* (Barnsley, 2010).
Repington, C. à C. *The First World War, 1914–1918: Personal Experiences of Lieut.-Col. C. à Court Repington* (London, 1920).
Schneider, W. and R. Strasheim, *Deutsche Kampfwagen Im 1. Weltkrieg: Der A7V und die Anfange deutscher Panzererentwicklung* (Friedberg, 1988).
Sheldon, J., *The German Army at Cambrai* (Barnsley, 2002).
Swinton, E.D., *Eyewitness: Being Personal Reminiscences of Certain Phases of the Great War, Including the Genesis of the Tank* (New York, 1972).
Strasheim, R., *Beute Tanks*, Vols 1 & 2 (Erlangen, 2011).
Stone, D., *The Kaiser's Army: The German Army in World War One* (London, 2015).
Strong, P. and S. Marble, *Artillery in the Great War* (Barnsley, 2014).
Turner, A., *Cambrai 1917: The Birth of Armoured Warfare* (Osprey Publishing, 2007).
Volckheim, E., *Die Kampfwagen in der heutigen Kriegsführung* (Berlin, 1924).
——, *Die deutschen Kampfwagen im Weltkriege* (Berlin, 1937).
——, *Deutsche Kampfwagen greifen an!: Erlebniffe eines Kampfwagenfeuhrers an der Westfront 1918* (Berlin, 1937).
Watson, W.H.L., *With The Tanks 1916–1918* (Barnsley, 2014).
Whaley, B., *Covert German Rearmament, 1919–1939: Deception and Misperception* (Maryland, 1984).
White, B.T., *Tanks and Other Fighting Vehicles 1900 to 1918* (London, 1970).
Zaloga, S., *German Panzers, 1914–1918* (Oxford, 2006).

Journals

Beach, J., 'British Intelligence and German Tanks, 1916–1918', *War in History*, Vol. 14, No. 4, 2007, pp. 454–75.
DiNardo, R.L., 'German Armour Doctrine: Correcting the Myths', *War in History*, Vol. 3, No. 4, 1996, pp. 384–97.

Kruger, R., 'German Tanks', *Army Ordnance*, July–August 1923, pp. 31–36.
Ralf Raths, 'German Tank Production and Armoured Warfare, 1916–18', *War and Society*, Vol. 30, No. 1, March 2011, pp. 24–47, (pp. 26–30).

Newspapers and Magazines

Anazc Bulletin, 10 May 1918, p. 10.
Anazc Bulletin, 20 September 1918, p. 1.
Anazc Bulletin, 19 July 1918, p. 2.
Anazc Bulletin, 26 July 1918, p. 3.
'German Tank Like Travelling Arsenal', *New York Times*, 30 March 1918, p. 2.
Robin Schäfer, 'The "Turncoat Armour" of WWI, The German Beutetank: Captured Tanks Used Against the Allies', *Iron Cross*, No. 7, 23 December 2020.
——, 'British Steel – Iron Cross', *Iron Cross*, No. 7, 23 December 2020.

Online Resources

https://api.parliament.uk/historic-hansard/commons/1916/oct/12/war-administration
https://tankmuseum.org/article/german-responses-tank
https://tankmuseum.org/article/action-debut-of-the-a7v-tank
https://tanks-encyclopedia.com
https://sites.google.com/site/landships/home
http://www.landships.info/landships/index.html

IN HAIG'S SHADOW

THE LETTERS OF MAJOR-GENERAL HUGO DE PREE AND FIELD MARSHAL SIR DOUGLAS HAIG

EDITED BY

GARY SHEFFIELD

Foreword by Janet, Lady Glover

A new airport parking garage that opened in 2021 provides a good vantage point for this view of a Red Line train composed of 1984-built Bombardier LRV 111 and 1998 Siemens car 246 leaving the airport station on what was still bidirectional single track, on June 3, 2023. The second pantograph on No. 111 was designed for clearing ice from the overhead wires during winter weather. (*Photograph by Steve Morgan*)

In 2023–2024, TriMet eliminated sections of two-way single track on the Red Line by laying a second track. The new track has yet to be equipped with overhead wire in this June 2023 photo showing a two-car train, consisting of two Type 5 Siemens S700 LRVs, leaving the airport. Trains would switch to the foreground track when it was opened in October 2023. (*Photograph by Steve Morgan*)

A new paint scheme introduced on buses in 2019 was slow to appear on MAX. However, dozens of LRVs received it in a short period in early 2024 after the agency decided to use an adhesive "wrap" instead of repainting. In May 2024, Nos. 301 and 315 are westbound on Holladay Street at 3rd Avenue, where the scene has changed since the 1990 photograph on page 117. (*Photograph by Steve Morgan*)

Elimination of the Red Line's single-track section, north of Gateway, required construction of an entirely new alignment for southbound trains, crossing over the now-northbound-only old alignment. It opened on March 4, 2024. On May 2, 2024, a train of SD660s, 319 and 208, is using the new line. I-205 is at left in this view from NE Halsey Street. (*Photograph by Steve Morgan*)

IMAGES OF WAR
BRANDENBURGER
WARTIME PHOTOGRAPHS OF
WILHELM WALTHER
ANTHONY ROGERS

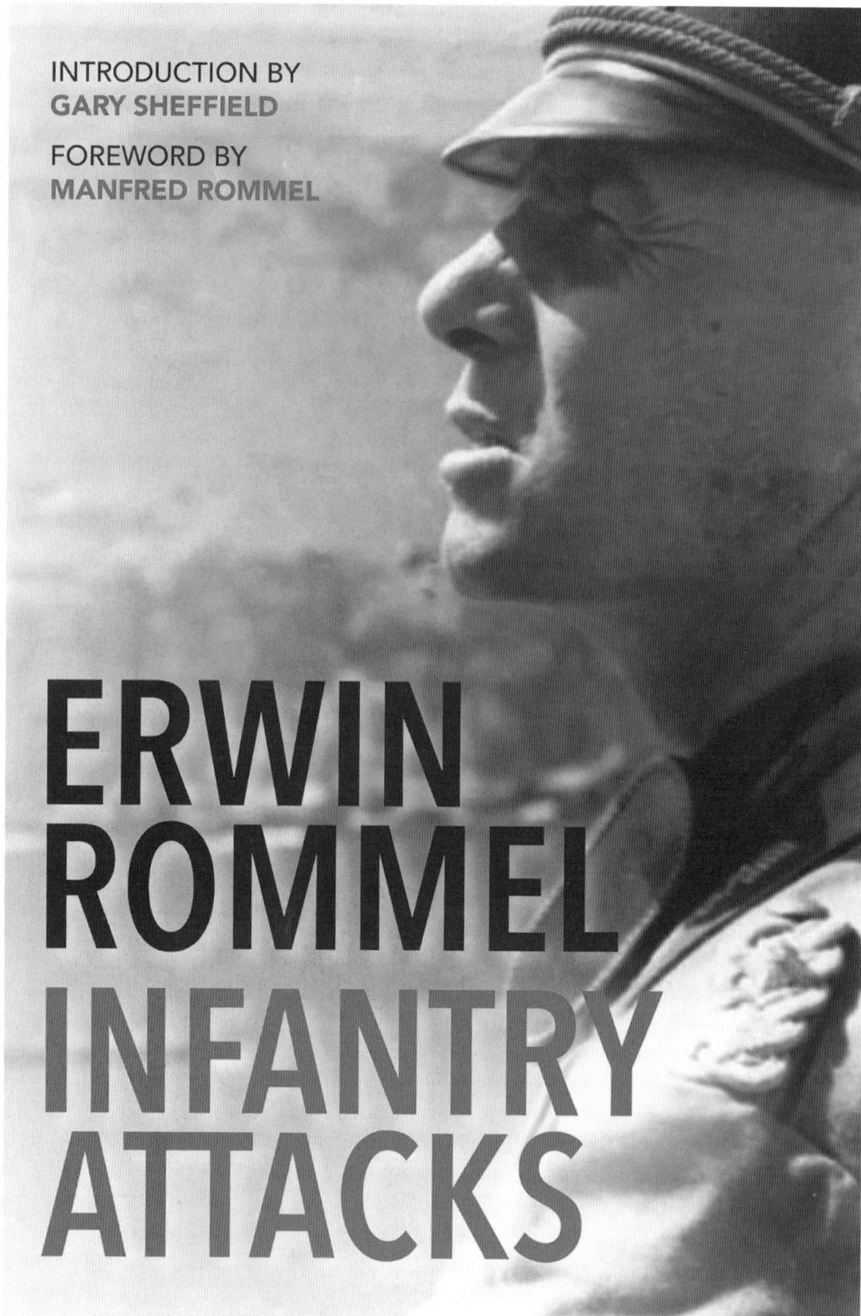
INTRODUCTION BY
GARY SHEFFIELD
FOREWORD BY
MANFRED ROMMEL
ERWIN
ROMMEL
INFANTRY
ATTACKS

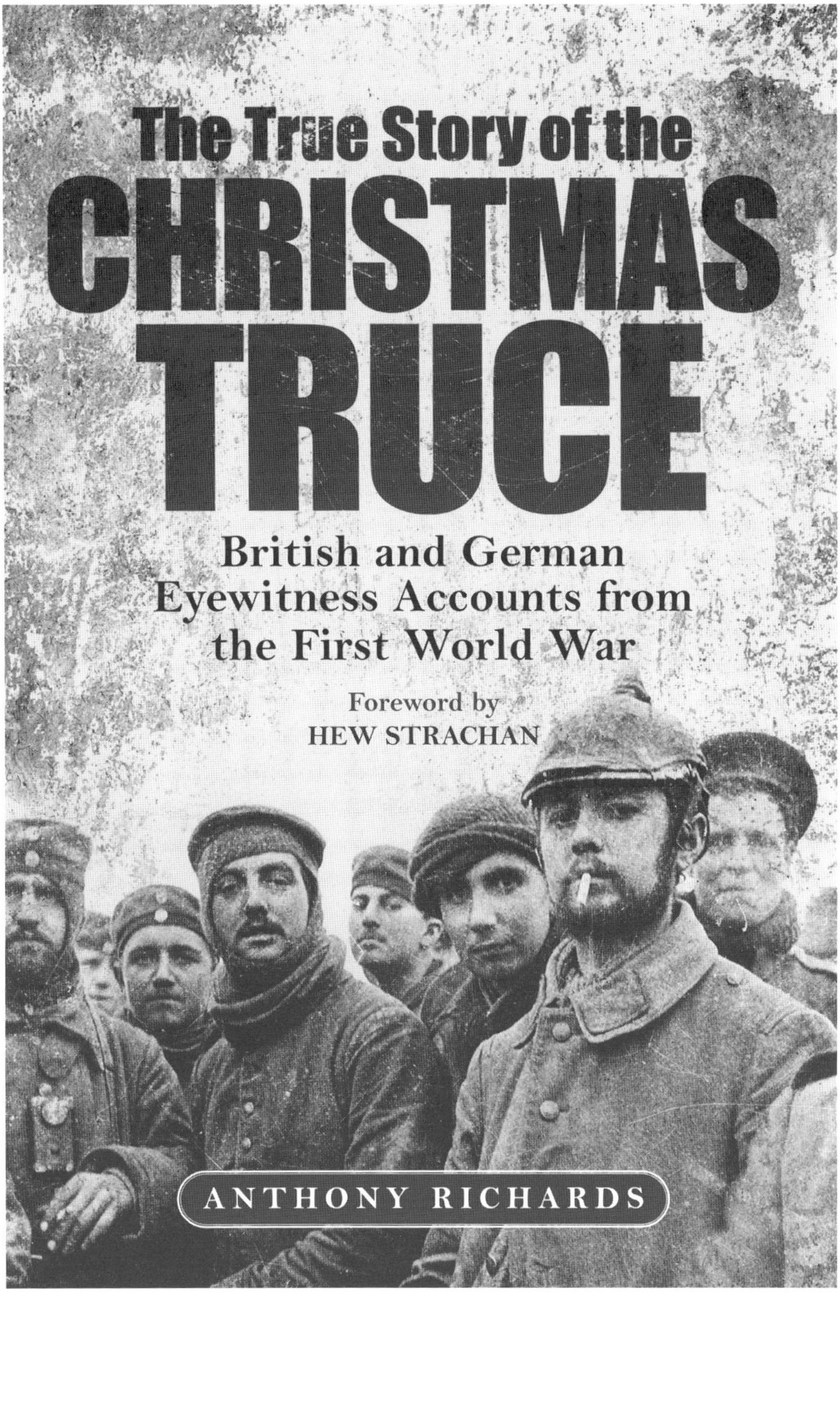
The True Story of the
CHRISTMAS
TRUCE
British and German
Eyewitness Accounts from
the First World War
Foreword by
HEW STRACHAN
ANTHONY RICHARDS

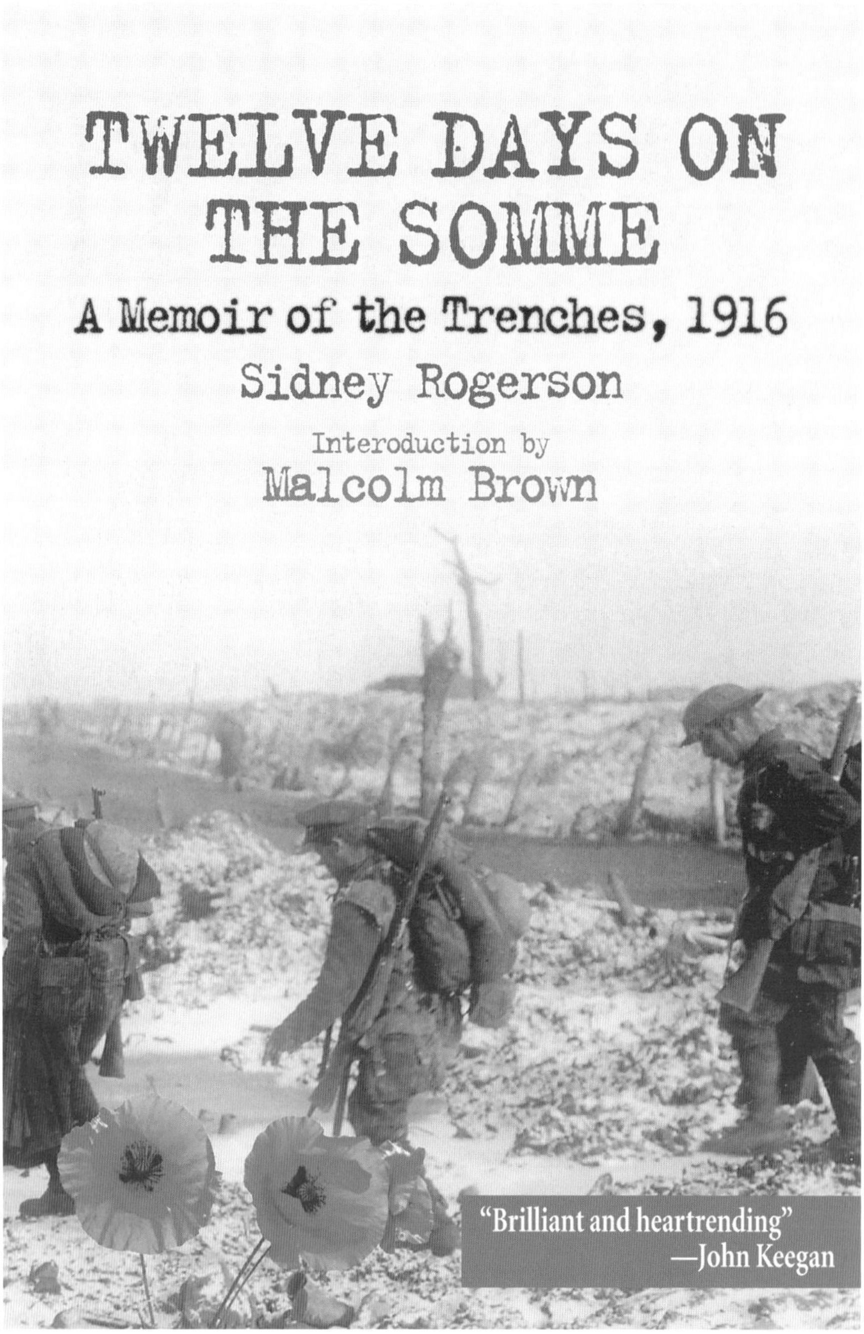
TWELVE DAYS ON THE SOMME
A Memoir of the Trenches, 1916
Sidney Rogerson
Interoduction by
Malcolm Brown
"Brilliant and heartrending"
—John Keegan

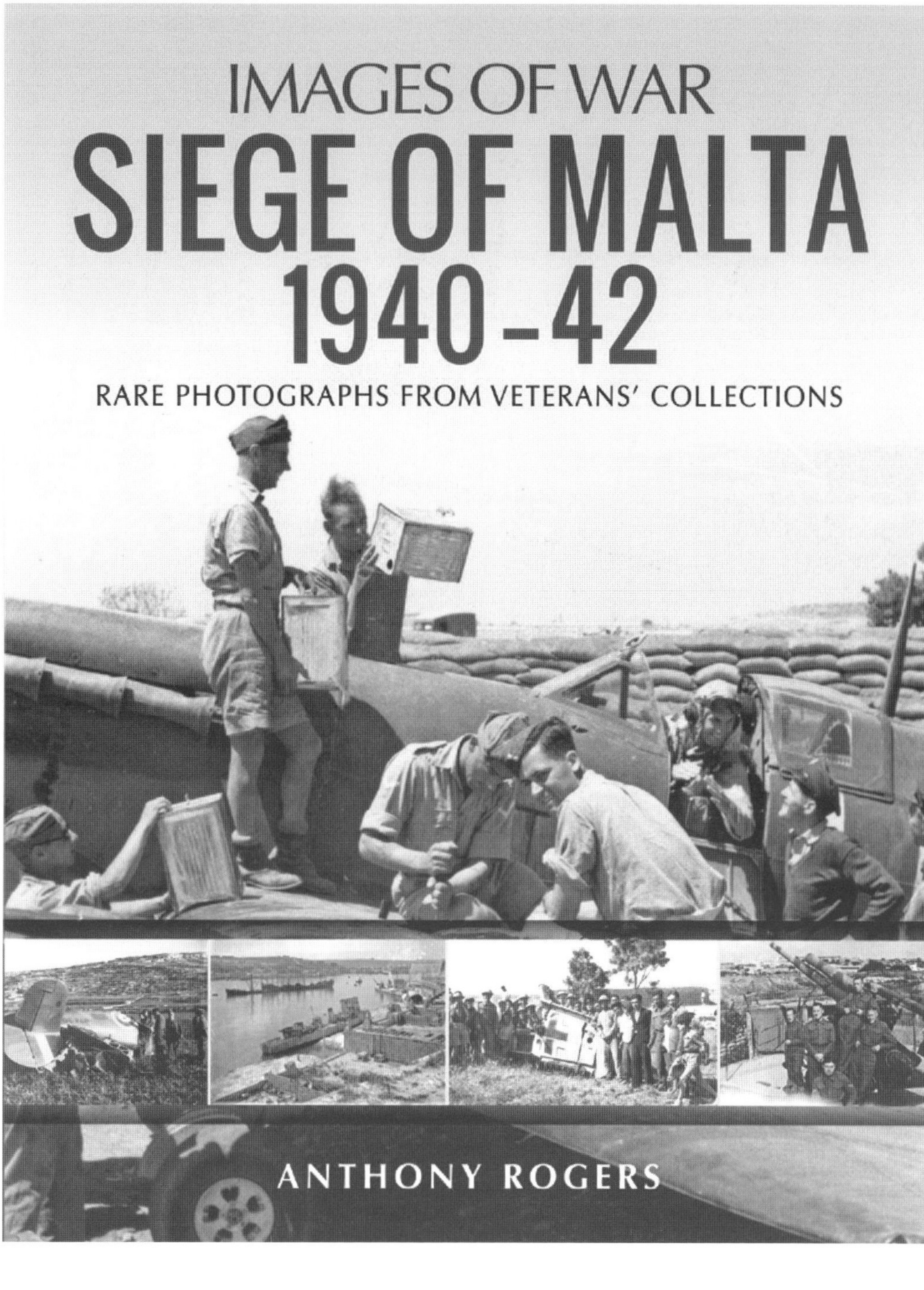
IMAGES OF WAR
SIEGE OF MALTA
1940–42
RARE PHOTOGRAPHS FROM VETERANS' COLLECTIONS
ANTHONY ROGERS

IMAGES OF WAR

STALAG LUFT III

THE GERMAN POW CAMP THAT INSPIRED *THE GREAT ESCAPE*

RARE PHOTOGRAPHS FROM WARTIME ARCHIVES

CHARLES MESSENGER